MANUAL

Fourth Edition

Procedures for the Office Professional

Patsy Fulton-Calkins, Ph.D., CPS
Adjunct Professor
Educational Consultant

Joanna D. Hanks
Dean of Instructional Services
J. Sargeant Reynolds Community College
Richmond, Virginia

Contributing Author

Karin M. Stultz
Northern Michigan University
Marquette, Michigan

VISIT US ON THE INTERNET
www.swep.com
www.thomsonlearning.com

South-Western
EDUCATIONAL PUBLISHING
Thomson Learning™

Australia • Canada • Denmark • Japan • Mexico • New Zealand • Philippines
Puerto Rico • Singapore • South Africa • Spain • United Kingdom • United States

Electronic Media
Limited Warranty

South-Western Educational Publishing ("South-Western") extends the following warranty to only the original customer:

Warranty Coverage
This warranty covers the media on which the South-Western software/data are recorded. This limited warranty does not extend to the information contained on the media and in the accompanying book materials (the "Software/data"). The media product is warranted against malfunction due to defective materials or construction. This warranty is void if the media product is damaged by accident or unreasonable use, neglect, installation, improper service, or other causes not arising out of defects in material or construction.

Warranty Duration
The media product is warranted for a period of three months from the date of the original purchase by the customer.

Warranty Disclaimers
The following should be read and understood before purchasing and/or using the media:

a. Any implied warranties that arise out of this sale are limited in duration to the above three-month period. South-Western will not be liable for loss of use of the media or other incidental or consequential costs, expenses, or damages incurred by you, the consumer, or any other user. Furthermore, South-Western will not be liable for any claim of any kind whatsoever by any other party against the user of the Software/data.

b. South-Western does not warrant that the Software/data and the media will be free from error or will meet the specific requirements of the consumer. You, the consumer, assume complete responsibility for any decisions made or actions taken based on information obtained using the Software/data.

c. Any statements made concerning the utility of the Software/data are not to be construed as expressed or implied warranties.

d. SOUTH-WESTERN MAKES NO WARRANTY, EITHER EXPRESSED OR IMPLIED, INCLUDING BUT NOT LIMITED TO ANY IMPLIED WARRANTY OR MERCHANTABILITY AND FITNESS FOR A PARTICULAR PURPOSE, REGARDING THE SOFTWARE/DATA AND MAKES ALL SOFTWARE/ DATA AVAILABLE SOLELY ON AN "AS IS" BASIS.

e. In no event will South-Western be liable to anyone for special collateral, incidental, or consequential damages in connection with or arising out of the purchase or use of the Software/data. The sole and exclusive liability of South-Western, regardless of the form of action, will not exceed the purchase price of the media.

f. Some states do not allow the exclusion or limitation of implied warranties or consequential damages, so the above limitations or exclusions may not apply to you in those states.

Further Disclaimers of Warranty
South-Western will extend no warranty where the software is used on a machine other than that designated on the software package.

Media Replacement
Provided that you, the customer, have satisfactorily completed and returned a copy of the License Agreement, South-Western will replace, during the warranty period, any defective media at no charge. At South-Western's option, the defective media must be returned, postage prepaid, along with proof of purchase date. Please contact South-Western at the address shown below for return instructions before returning any defective media.

South-Western Educational Publishing
Media Services
5101 Madison Road
Cincinnati, OH 45227

Legal Remedies
This warranty gives you specific legal rights, and you may also have other rights that vary from state to state.

Technical Support Hotline

The Technical Support Hotline (800/543-0453) is available to help you with any technical problems you may be having with this media product.

If you identify a problem, please check your hardware to make sure it is working properly. If the hardware is functioning correctly, call the number given. Please have the following information and materials with you when calling the hotline:

- program or template diskette or CD-ROM
- text
- instructor's manual

- list of any error messages
- students' printouts
- description of the problem
- computer type and model
- computer's memory configuration
- version number of operating system
- name and version number of commercial software (if applicable)

Please do not permit your students access to the hotline number. If you want to order software, call (800) 354-9706. If you need product information, call (800) 824-5179.

SPECIAL NOTE TO INSTRUCTORS

If you assign the following **Office Applications** to your students, ask them to do the following:

OA2-1   Save the memorandum form on the student template disk in file OA02-1b so that it may be used again in later Office Applications. The memorandum form may be saved easily by doing the following:
  a. After printing out the job for OA2-1, close out the screen.
  b. When asked if changes are to be saved to file OA02-1b, respond "no." There will then be a clean memorandum form to be used again in Office Applications OA2-5, OA7-3, ORA10-5, OA12-1, and OA15-4.

OA2-5   Use the memorandum form on the student template disk in file OA02-1b; follow the same procedure given previously to save a blank form.

OA7-3   Use the memorandum form on the student template disk in file OA02-1b; follow the same procedure given previously to save a blank form.

ORA10-5   Use the memorandum form on the disk in file OA02-1b; follow the same procedure given previously to save a blank form.

ORA12-1   Use the memorandum form on the disk in file OA02-1b; follow the same procedure given previously to save a blank form.

OA15-4   Use the memorandum form on the disk in file OA02-1b; follow the same procedure given previously to save a blank memorandum form.

OA10-3   Save the letterhead on the student template disk in file OA10-3 to be used again in the Office Application OA11-1 and Supplemental Exercise 11. Save the letterhead form using the same instructions as given above to save the memorandum form.

OA11-1   Use the letterhead on the student template disk in file OA10-3. Follow the same procedure to save the letterhead form as a new form for use in Supplemental Exercise 11.

Supplemental
Exercise Use the letterhead on the student template disk in file OA10-3.

Note: Version 2.0 of the template disk can be downloaded from www.swep.com. From the Keyboarding & Office Tech. web page, click on the Resources link. Should problems occur, call the Technical Support Hotline (800/543-0453) for a replacement disk.

If you assign the following **Office Applications** to your students and you prefer to download Version 2.0 of the template disk, make copies of the template disk for your students and ask them to do the following:

OA6-2   Use the memorandum form on the student template disk in file OA06-2 rather than OA02-1b as listed in the textbook.

OA6-3   Use the memorandum form on the student template disk in file OA06-3 rather than OA02-1b as listed in the textbook.

OA6-6   Use the memorandum form on the student template disk in file OA06-6 rather than OA02-1b as listed in the textbook.

OA7-1   Use the memorandum form on the student template disk in file OA07-1 rather than OA02-1b as listed in the textbook.

Contents

PART 4:   RECORDS MANAGEMENT

PART 5:   MEETINGS, TRAVEL, AND FINANCIAL DOCUMENTS

PART 6:   THE OFFICE PROFESSIONAL'S CAREER

Preface

TO THE INSTRUCTOR

Procedures for the Office Professional is a comprehensive textbook containing 6 parts and 20 chapters. These additional materials are included to assist the student in the learning process:

- An Applications Workbook
- A student template disk containing office applications, letterhead, and forms
- Six achievement tests correlated with the six parts of the textbook
- Presentation software that emphasizes key concepts from each chapter

Each chapter of the textbook has a list of goals that follow the introductory paragraph. Each chapter concludes with seven reinforcement activities:

- A succinct **Summary** of the chapter
- **Key Terms** listed in the order they are presented in the chapter
- **Professional Pointers** that provide tips to help the student succeed
- **Office Procedures Reinforcement** that gives five questions/items for the student to complete
- **Critical Thinking Activity** that presents an office case for the student to analyze
- **Office Applications** tied directly to the goals of the chapter and designed to reinforce learning
- **Online Research Applications** in which the student uses the Internet

In addition, at the end of each of the six parts of the textbook, a **Vocabulary Review** and a **Language Skills Practice** are given in the Applications Workbook.

NEW FEATURES

Several new features are in this edition; they are listed here.

- An integrated learning system that includes:
  —Learning activities tied directly to goals
  —Emphasis on critical thinking and team building skills throughout the text
  —Activities that support critical thinking and team building skills
  —Emphasis on technical skills, with template disk activities that give the student practical experience in using technology

  —End-of-part tests that include as an option a case for students to solve as a team
- New chapter—Chapter 8: The Virtual Environment
- Online research applications through the use of the Internet
- Office simulation application (with an international focus) in the Applications Workbook
- An expanded instructor's manual

TEXT ORGANIZATION

Procedures for the Office Professional is organized into 6 parts, with a total of 20 chapters. These parts and chapters are:

PART 1: THE 21st CENTURY OFFICE
    Chapter 1: A Changing Workplace
    Chapter 2: The Office Team and Environment
    Chapter 3: Productivity in the Office
    Chapter 4: Ethical Behavior

PART 2: OFFICE TECHNOLOGY
    Chapter 5: Information Processing
    Chapter 6: Computer Software
    Chapter 7: Reprographic Resources
    Chapter 8: The Virtual Office

PART 3: OFFICE COMMUNICATION
    Chapter 9: The Communication Process
    Chapter 10: Written Communications
    Chapter 11: Presentations
    Chapter 12: Telecommunication Skills
    Chapter 13: Office Mail

PART 4: RECORDS MANAGEMENT
    Chapter 14: Rules and Procedures
    Chapter 15: Records Management Technology

PART 5: MEETINGS, TRAVEL, AND FINANCIAL DOCUMENTS
    Chapter 16: Meetings and Conferences
    Chapter 17: Travel Arrangements
    Chapter 18: Financial Documents

PART 6: THE OFFICE PROFESSIONAL'S CAREER
    Chapter 19: Employment and Advancement
    Chapter 20: Leadership and Management

SUGGESTED OUTLINE FOR A 16-WEEK COURSE

You may teach the class in one, two, or three sessions each week. This plan assumes that the material covered each week will be the same regardless of the number of times the class meets each week.

LEARNING THEORY EMPHASIS

The textbook and supplementary materials have been written using sound learning theory. Student mastery of the material is encouraged through the following elements.

Chapter Goals

Effective instructional theory demands that students understand what they are expected to learn. Goals are stated succinctly at the beginning of each chapter, following the introductory paragraph(s). Each end-of-chapter activity is one step in a nine-step process for the student in achieving the goals.

Step 1: Read the text, paying particular attention to the goals that are to be achieved.

Step 2: Read the chapter Summary.

Step 3: Read the Key Terms, being certain that the definition of the terms can be reiterated.

Step 4: Complete the Office Procedures Reinforcement items.

Step 5: Read and respond to the items given in the Critical Thinking Activity.

Step 6: Complete the Office Applications.

Step 7: Complete the Online Research Applications.

Step 8: Demonstrate knowledge through completion of part tests.

Step 9: Demonstrate skill attainment through the Simulated Office Application.

Each end-of-chapter activity is explained in more detail in the next section.

Summary

A chapter summary highlighting briefly the important points of each chapter is given at the end of the chapter. The summary provides a quick review for the student on the main points of the chapter. After reading the summary, the student may want to review any part of the chapter that he or she does not understand.

Key Terms

Key terms are highlighted throughout each chapter and then listed in order of appearance at the end of each chapter. This approach allows students to check quickly to determine if they know the definition of the key terms. If not, they can go back and review the definitions within the chapter.

Office Procedures Reinforcement

Five items to which the student must respond with short answers are given at the end of each chapter. In responding to these items, you may have the students work individually, work in teams, write the responses, or respond through class discussions.

Critical Thinking Activity

Cases involving office situations are given, with items to which the student must respond at the end of each case. You may ask students to do these cases individually or as a team. Also, you may ask them to write their responses or to present them orally in a class discussion.

Office Applications

Each office application is tied to one of the goals given at the beginning of the chapter. The goal number is placed in parentheses next to the office application number. Some applications cover more than one goal. This approach allows you, as the instructor, to delete goals at the beginning of the chapter if you desire and then to also delete the activity or activities that correspond to the goal.

Online Research Applications

Since the Internet is used so extensively today, office applications that require the student to use it are given. These activities are also tied to one of the goals of the chapter. However, an unstated goal is to familiarize the student with the numerous data sources that are available on the Internet.

Icons

You will notice that two types of icons are used: team building and template disk.

STUDENT TEMPLATE DISK

A student template disk comes packaged with the text. The disk includes activities, forms, and letterhead. The student is told in the activity which file to access on the template disk.

PROFESSIONAL POINTERS

Professional pointers are given at the end of each chapter. These pointers give the student some additional tips for being effective as an office professional in the twenty-first century world.

SUPPLEMENTAL EXERCISES

A supplemental exercise is provided for each chapter. An explanation of the exercise and the key appear in the Instructor's Manual. The exercise for the student appears in the Applications Workbook. If you determine that you want to assign the exercise, you will need to give the student information as to where it can be found. The Applications Workbook page numbers are given here.

Supplemental Exercise	Applications Workbook Page Number(s)
Chapter 1	5–9
Chapter 2	14
Chapter 3	25–26
Chapter 4	27
Chapter 5	39–40
Chapter 6	44
Chapter 7	49–50
Chapter 8	51
Chapter 9	59
Chapter 10	63–67
Chapter 11	71
Chapter 12	77
Chapter 13	81
Chapter 14	93
Chapter 15	100–101
Chapter 16	109
Chapter 17	114
Chapter 18	125
Chapter 19	136
Chapter 20	139

END-OF-PART ACTIVITIES

At the end of each of the six parts, the students are given a Vocabulary Review and a Language Skills Practice to complete in the Applications Workbook. The parts and the chapters they cover are:

Part 1—Chapters 1–4
Part 2—Chapters 5–8
Part 3—Chapters 9–13
Part 4—Chapters 14–15
Part 5—Chapters 16–18
Part 6—Chapters 19–20

The Vocabulary Review consists of identifying key terms that are presented in the chapters. The Language Skills Practice covers English usage rules that are presented in the Reference Section of the text. Students may need to review the Reference Section before completing the sentences.

TEXT REFERENCE SECTION

In the appendix of the text there is a Reference Section covering a review of English fundamentals, plus a section on business introductions. The parts are:

- Abbreviations
- Capitalization
- Numbers
- Often Misused Words and Phrases
- Plurals and Possessives
- Punctuation
- Proofreaders' Marks
- Spelling
- Word Division
- Proper Business Introductions

ELECTRONIC PRESENTATION SOFTWARE

Electronic presentation software is available from South-Western. To order, use ISBN 0-538-72214-2. The software provides material, by chapter, for group instruction similar to the way transparencies or slides would be used as a lecture aid. The software is presented in chapter order, with goals for each chapter presented as the first section.

SIMULATED OFFICE APPLICATION

A Simulated Office Application is given as the last section of the Applications Workbook. Simulated activities occur over a period of five days. Additional information and forms for the student are given on the student template disk. You may want to use this activity as a final exam for the student. It provides practical application of many of the concepts presented in the text. Also, you may want the students to work in teams of two or three as they complete this activity.

TESTS

A CD-ROM containing six achievement tests (one covering each part of the textbook) is furnished free of charge to institutions using *Procedures for the Office Professional*. Each test consists of true-false, matching, and short-answer items. There is also an optional case provided on each test. Throughout the text, team building has been stressed. You may assign the case as a team building exercise, allowing two or three students to work together on the completion of the items given at the end of the case. The point value on the case is 20; however, you may adjust the point value of the test to achieve a total of 100 points. Through the testing software, the instructor has the ability to create a printed test and/or exam from preferred text questions. You will be able to determine which questions to choose and the order for the questions. To request the CD-ROM, order ISBN 0-538-72217-7.

INSTRUCTIONAL SUGGESTIONS

As you think about how you want to teach this course, here are several suggestions.

Present the Goals of the Course to the Student

In addition to the chapter goals that are given in the text, you may want to present the goals of the course to the student on the first day of class. Here are suggested course goals.

- Develop the skills and knowledge needed for:
  — the twenty-first century office
  — working effectively with teams
  — controlling time and stress
  — behaving ethically in the workplace
- Develop technical skills to work successfully with:
  — computer hardware
  — computer software
  — reprographics
  — virtual situations
- Develop an understanding of the communication process and skills in:
  — oral communication
  — written communication
  — presenting before groups
- Effectively handle:
  — office mail
  — records management
  — meetings and conferences
  — travel arrangements
  — financial documents
- Develop skills in finding and advancing on a job
- Develop leadership skills

You might want to stress to the students that this course builds on skills where they already have some expertise, expands their expertise, and helps them get ready to enter the workforce or improve their skills if they are presently in the workforce. For example, most students will have taken an introductory computer course before taking this course. The concepts presented in Chapter 5 review some of the information they have already learned and present some new information.

Review the Textbook and Ancillary Materials With the Student

Help the student learn how to use the textbook and ancillary materials by reviewing:

- Goals at the beginning of each chapter
- End-of-chapter activities, including:
  — Summary
  — Key Terms
  — Office Procedures Reinforcement
  — Critical Thinking Activity
  — Office Applications and Online Research Applications
  — Professional Pointers
- End-of-part activities:
  — Vocabulary Review
  — Language Skills Practice, calling attention to the Reference Section in the textbook as a help in completing the items

Assist the Students With Developing Team Building Skills

The word "team" can be traced back to the Indo-European word "deuk" (to pull); it has always included a meaning of "pulling together."[1] Here are several suggestions for assisting your students as they develop team building skills.

- Basic interpersonal skills are essential in team building; begin team building activities after Chapter 2—The Office Team and Environment. When Chapter 9 is discussed, emphasize the importance of communication in the team building process. Stress the following:
  — One-on-one communication
  — Group communication
  — Listening
  — Questioning
  — Feedback
  — Conflict resolution
  — Group problem solving
  — Evaluating team performance—an evaluation form may be developed for team members to evaluate how the team is working
  — Using the evaluation to build a more solid team

There are a number of books on team building that you may want to review. Ury's *Getting Past No* (written to assist in making the negotiation process more humane) has numerous helpful hints for building working teams, some of which are:

- Listen actively
- Express views without provoking
- Ask problem-solving questions

---

[1]Peter M. Senge, Art Kleiner, Charlotte Roberts, Richard B. Ross, and Bryan J. Smith, *The Fifth Discipline Fieldbook* (New York: Doubleday, 1994), 354.

- Ask for constructive criticism
- Build bridges to agreement[2]

The Dartnell Corporation publishes a newsletter entitled *Teamwork* that gives many helpful suggestions concerning building teams. The phone number is 800-621-5463, email: *teamwk@dartnellcorp.com.*

Assist the Students With Developing Critical Thinking Skills

Richard Paul, in his book *Critical Thinking: How to Prepare Students for a Rapidly Changing World* defines critical thinking as: a unique kind of purposeful thinking in which the thinker systematically and habitually:

- Imposes criteria and intellectual standards upon the thinking by identifying criteria of solid reasoning such as precision, relevance, accuracy, sufficiency, and establishing a clear standard by which the effectiveness of the thinking will be finally assessed
- Takes charge of the construction of thinking by being aware of the elements of thought such as assumptions and points of view
- Guides the construction of the thinking according to standards by continually assessing the process, adjusting, adapting, and improving
- Assesses the effectiveness of the thinking according to the purpose, the criteria, and the standards

Questions one might ask when thinking critically about issues include:

- Is this belief/idea/concept defensible or indefensible?
- Is my position on this issue reasonable and rational?
- Am I willing to deal with complexity or do I retreat into simple stereotypes to avoid it?
- If I can't tell if my idea or belief is reasonable or defensible, how can I have confidence in my thinking?
- Is it appropriate and wise to assume that my ideas and beliefs are accurate, clear, and reasonable when I haven't really tested them?
- What assumptions am I making; what am I taking for granted?
- Am I thinking deeply or only on the surface about the issue?
- Do I ever enter sympathetically into points of view that are very different from my own, or do I just assume that I am right?
- Do I know how to question my own ideas and to test them?
- Are my conclusions defensible?
- What would the consequences be if I acted on my beliefs about the subject being considered?[3]

Using Community Resources

Teaching suggestions are given in each chapter, with outside speakers identified as an effective resource. Such speakers can provide an additional viewpoint on a topic and add their own personal experiences to reinforce their views. If you are using speakers, these suggestions can help you in the planning process.

- When contacting the potential speaker, explain the purpose of the visit. Let the speaker know what objectives are important to cover in the session.
- Give the speaker some background about the students—their knowledge of the subject, their experience, the age ranges, and the number of students in the class.
- Determine if the speaker needs any equipment during the presentation.
- Arrange to have someone meet the speaker if the person is unfamiliar with the building; send a map of the location to the speaker.
- Provide the speaker with a written confirmation of the date, time, and location for the presentation.
- Prepare the students for the presentation. You may want to have the students prepare questions for the speaker in advance.
- Get a resume from the speaker. Arrange to have someone introduce the speaker; one of your students can learn from the experience.
- If you desire to audiotape or videotape the presentation, obtain permission in advance from the speaker. If the speaker grants permission, the taping should be done as inconspicuously as possible.
- Arrange for any publicity desired. You may want to notify the local papers or your school paper of the event.
- Write a thank-you note to the speaker and also ask that your students (as a class) write a thank-you note.
- Provide follow-up of the presentation through a discussion with your students during the next class period. Summarize the important points.

COMPANY ORIENTATION

In the preface to the Applications Workbook, the students are given information about a company for whom they will be working. To reinforce the international nature of many companies today, the company, *People First International,* operates from a home office in Detroit, Michigan, with other offices in New York City, New York; Atlanta, Georgia; Paris, France; and Frankfurt, Germany. Information about the company and the position the student has is provided. Many of the activities within the text and the workbook refer to this company. The letterhead and memorandum forms provided also reflect this company orientation.

A PERSONAL NOTE

As the authors, we have thoroughly enjoyed writing this textbook and the ancillary materials. It is our hope that your students learn from this book and that you enjoy facilitating their learning and growth. We wish you and your students every success.

---

[2]William Ury, *Getting Past No* (New York: Bantam, 1991).
[3]Richard Paul, *Critical Thinking: How to Prepare Students for a Rapidly Changing World* (Santa Rosa, CA: Foundation for Critical Thinking, 1995).

Part 1: The 21st Century Office

CHAPTER 1

A CHANGING WORKPLACE

The workplace of the twenty-first century promises to change at a rapid pace due to major technological advances and the international nature of our world. This chapter introduces the changes expected in the work environment, plus possible career opportunities and skills needed. The student is also introduced to setting goals and making effective decisions.

STUDENT GOALS

1. Describe the forces that are changing the office environment.
2. Identify career opportunities in the office field.
3. Define the skills and knowledge needed to succeed in the office.
4. Develop a career plan with short- and long-range goals.
5. Engage in effective decision making.

CHAPTER OUTLINE

   I. Introduction
  II. Your Goals
 III. The Information Age Office
     A. Increasingly Diverse Labor Force
     B. Increased Education
     C. Changing Businesses
        1. Multinational Corporations
        2. Quality Focus
        3. Flattened Organizational Structure
        4. Flexible Workweek
        5. The Virtual Office
        6. Contracted Specialists
 IV. Career Opportunities
     A. Types of Positions Available
        1. Technical
        2. Health Occupations
        3. Legal
        4. Education
        5. Travel and Tourism
        6. Salaries
     B. Twenty-First Century Skills
        1. Communication Skills
        2. Human Relations Skills
        3. Time and Organizational Management Skills
        4. Critical Thinking Skills
        5. Decision-Making Skills
        6. Creative Thinking Skills
        7. Technology Skills
        8. Lifelong-Learning Skills
  V. Your Career Path
     A. Set Appropriate Goals
     B. Make Effective Decisions
        1. Define the Problem or the Purpose
        2. Establish the Criteria
        3. Generate Alternatives or Possible Solutions
        4. Test the Alternatives and Make the Decision
        5. Evaluate the Decision
  V. Summary
 VI. Key Terms
 VII. Professional Pointers
VIII. Office Procedures Reinforcement
 IX. Critical Thinking Activity
  X. Office Applications
 XI. Online Research Applications

TEACHING SUGGESTIONS

Since this chapter is the introductory chapter and the students probably do not know each other and may not have been in one of your classes previously, it is a good idea to spend some time in initial get-acquainted activities. These activities should include an introduction to the course and to you as the instructor, along with a chance for them to learn more about their classmates.

• Give the students an overview of the course and what you expect of them. Material is provided in the introductory pages of this manual, giving the overall goals for the course. You will probably want to give them a syllabus detailing these objectives, your attendance policy, grading policy, and other expectations that you have.

1

- At the end of many of the chapters, there are activities where the student is expected to interview individuals or seek out special types of information within the community. The students probably will not have a thorough knowledge of the business community. One way to help them understand more about it is to invite in a local official (such as the city manager, mayor, or chamber of commerce executive) to give them an overview of the major businesses in the area, the strategic plans for the city or community, and so forth.
- One concept presented in Chapter 1 is the continuing diversity of our population and our workforce. A human resource executive from one of the larger companies in your community may be invited to discuss the diversity of the workforce.
- To help students get to know each other more quickly, ask them to work in teams on certain assignments. One activity,

ORA 1-6, provides for teamwork. You might also ask the students to work in teams on the Office Procedures Reinforcement questions and the Critical Thinking Activity.

KEY TO SUPPLEMENTAL EXERCISE

An additional office assignment is provided in the Applications Workbook. The student is given information on the training and qualifications needed for clerical supervisors and managers, court reporters and medical transcriptionists, record clerks and secretaries. The student is to review the information and prepare in columnar form the training and qualifications needed for each area. The student is to provide an appropriate title for the summary and submit a copy of the report to you. Although student responses will vary, here is a possible solution.

TRAINING AND QUALIFICATIONS FOR SPECIALIZED OCCUPATIONS

Training	Qualifications
Clerical Supervisors and Managers	
Postsecondary training, with an associate's degree or bachelor's degree required in some jobs	Teamwork skills
	Determination
	Loyalty
	Confidence
	Ability to organize and coordinate work, establish priorities, and motivate others
	Broad base of office skills
	Ability to adapt to change
	Attention to detail
	Working knowledge of computers
Court Reporters	
Postsecondary training in a two- or four-year program	Ability to capture dictation at 225 words per minute
Certified Court Reporter designation	Excellent English grammar and punctuation skills
Notary Public certification	Computer proficiency
	Listening skills
Medical Transcriptionists	
Postsecondary training in medical transcription	Good English grammar and punctuation skills
Completion of two-year associate degree program	Proficiency with computers and word processing software
Coursework in anatomy, medical terminology, medical/legal issues, and	Listening skills
English grammar and punctuation	
Certification through the American Association for Medical Transcriptionists	
Record Clerks	
High school diploma or equivalent, with postsecondary education usually favored	Computer proficiency
	Knowledge of word processing and spreadsheet software
	Interpersonal skills
	Careful, orderly, and detail-oriented
	Honest, discreet, and trustworthy
	Strong aptitude for numbers
Secretaries	
High school graduate	Keyboarding proficiency
Business school, vocational-technical school, or community college graduate	Spelling, punctuation, grammar, and oral communication skills
	Knowledge of word processing, spreadsheet, and database management programs
	Good interpersonal skills
	Discretion, judgment, organizational ability, and initiative

KEY TO OFFICE PROCEDURES REINFORCEMENT

1. Define and explain the following terms:

   a. Virtual environment

      Technology has spawned the virtual concept, meaning that through technology an individual may be physically in one location and virtually present at another. Virtual situations can vary significantly. The most common example consists of the individual worker who is equipped with a laptop, notebook, or handheld computer for traveling; a cellular phone; pager; fax machine; email; and voice mail system, with the workplace varying. The employee may work at the company office for a portion of a day or a week and at his or her home for the remainder of the time. Or the employee may work exclusively from the home. The individual may be employed by a company or be self-employed.

   b. Information Age

      The Information Age is defined as the age of great explosion of knowledge. One of the results of this age is an increase in the amount of information available to us. Technology is an integral part of the Information Age.

   c. Digital era

      The digital era is part of the Information Age; technology has spawned the digital era—a world fueled by numbers. In this world, we wallow in numbers—account numbers, credit card numbers, personal identification numbers, and so forth. The invention that unleashed the digital era is the microchip—a device the size of a fingernail that empowers our technological equipment.

2. Describe four characteristics of the labor force of 2006.

   - The number of Hispanics and Asians in the workforce will increase.
   - The number of women in the workforce will increase.
   - Workers over 45 will account for a larger share of the labor force.
   - More immigrants will be in the workforce.
   - The workforce will have increasing levels of education.

3. List four ways in which the office environment is changing.

   The student may list any of these ways:

   - Types of businesses changing, with the service and professional specialty occupations growing faster than other areas of the job market
   - Businesses operating with fewer employees and flatter organizational structures
   - An increased focus on quality, with high standards of performance essential

   - More flexibility in the workweek, with increasing numbers of individuals working in virtual environment situations
   - More contracted specialists
   - Increased multinational corporations

4. Explain the difference between a hierarchy and a flattened organizational structure.

   A hierarchy is organized according to rank or authority. Such a structure assumes that knowledge and information flow from the top down—from the president or CEO of the company to the workers. In the Information Age this organizational structure is less effective than in the past. The president or CEO cannot have all of the knowledge or information necessary to produce the product or service; our world is too complex. The flattened organizational structure has fewer levels than the traditional structure, and individuals tend to work in teams. For example, within a workgroup there may be 25 to 30 people reporting to one individual. However, these individuals may work in teams of five or six members on particular projects, with the projects changing as the demands of the organization change.

5. List six skills required of the office professional; explain their importance.

   The student may list any of these skills:

   - Communication skills
   - Human relations skills
   - Time and organizational management skills
   - Critical thinking skills
   - Decision-making skills
   - Creative thinking skills
   - Technology skills
   - Lifelong-learning skills

   As the workforce becomes more diverse, the use of technology continues to increase, and there are increased quality performance expectations. The office professional must be able to communicate well with all individuals within the office and the customers or clients. The office professional must work with teams of people in getting the job done and produce work quickly, using the technology that is available. He or she must be able to evaluate situations and make good decisions, while producing quality products. All of these demands require the skills mentioned above.

KEY TO CRITICAL THINKING ACTIVITY

Although the answers to the questions in this activity will vary, here are suggested responses.

1. List the experiences and achievements that Carlotta has had that affect her career plan.

   - Good grade point average in high school
   - President of the Student Government

• Work experience as a receptionist in a community college, with excellent evaluations by her supervisors

2. What steps might Carlotta take to enhance her chances of achieving her short- and long-term goals?

   • Begin work on her associate degree; maintain a high grade point average; determine whether she can afford to go to school full-time or whether she must maintain her job full-time and go to school part-time
   • Become active in selected extracurricular activities; strive to obtain a leadership role in certain activities
   • Whether she is working full- or part-time, be willing to accept challenging work assignments to broaden her knowledge
   • Develop a plan of action for completing her college work
   • While in school begin to research positions available in the legal field

3. What skills should Carlotta develop to ensure success in the legal field? How should she go about developing these skills?

   • Computer proficiency
   • Software proficiency
   • Communication skills
   • Time and organizational management skills
   • Critical thinking skills
   • Decision-making skills
   • Creative thinking skills
   • Lifelong-learning skills

Carlotta should develop these skills by applying herself in her courses in school, by willingly taking on challenging opportunities on the job, and by becoming active in extracurricular activities in school.

KEY TO OFFICE APPLICATIONS

OA1-1 (Goals 1 and 3)

The student is asked to interview three office professionals who are currently in the field. The student may choose to do these interviews through email if access exists. These questions are to be asked of the professional:

• How long have you worked as an office professional?
• What changes in the office environment have you seen since you began working?
• How have you handled these changes?
• What skills do you need to be effective on your job?
• How do you keep current in your field?
• What are the advantages/disadvantages of your current position?
• What advice would you give to a student to help prepare for the same type of career that you have?

The student is to write a summary of his or her findings, giving the names of the office professionals interviewed and

their company affiliation. The summary is to be presented orally to the class and submitted to you. Thank-you letters are to be written to the office professionals.

OA 1-2 (Goal 1)

The student is to use the information presented in the Applications Workbook to prepare a chart showing graphically the percent of the labor force by race from 1996 and projected through 2006.

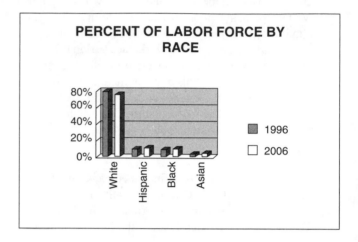

OA 1-3 (Goal 2)

The student is asked to research for three weeks the job openings that are listed in the classified ad section of the Sunday paper. A list is to be compiled of these openings by the type of business. The entry salaries (if given) and the qualifications required for the job are to be compiled. The findings are to be presented orally to the class and submitted in writing to you.

OA 1-4 (Goal 3)

The student is to use the self-evaluation chart provided on page 3 of the Applications Workbook to rate himself/herself on strengths and weaknesses. The evaluation is then to be discussed with a trusted friend, coworker, or family member to see if the person agrees with the ratings. The self-evaluation is to be kept, and the student is to rate himself/herself again at the end of the course to determine if strengths have been increased and weaknesses lessened. This self-evaluation is not to be submitted to you.

OA 1-5 (Goals 4 and 5)

The student is to prepare a career plan, noting the current status of his or her career and the goals expected to be achieved in three years, detailing plans for accomplishing the goals. Also, the student is to note career expectations in ten years and the projected means of accomplishing these goals. A copy of the career plan outline is to be submitted to you; the student is also to keep a copy and make changes (if appropriate) during the semester.

KEY TO ONLINE RESEARCH APPLICATIONS

ORA 1-6 (Goal 1)

The student is to select two or three classmates to work with on this project. Using the Internet, the student is to research what is happening with the virtual office; for example, the numbers of individuals who are employed virtually and in what capacity. A synopsis of the findings is to be submitted to you and presented orally to the class.

ORA 1-7 (Goal 2)

The student is to check the Internet for office positions that are available. The listing is to be printed and submitted to you.

CHAPTER 2

THE OFFICE TEAM AND ENVIRONMENT

The two major factors that influence productivity and happiness on the job are the relationships that individuals have with the people with whom they work and the physical environment in which they work. This chapter helps the student understand how to work effectively with the workplace team and how to be safe and physically healthy in the office. The student is expected to accomplish the following goals.

STUDENT GOALS

1. Demonstrate how to work effectively with internal and external teams.
2. Demonstrate how to be effective with office visitors.
3. Describe and engage in productive communication.
4. Describe the role of ergonomics, safety, and health in the office.

CHAPTER OUTLINE

TEACHING SUGGESTIONS

Since the ability to work well in teams is so important, you may want to have students work in teams on all assignments in this chapter. The assignments are written so that you may easily assign them as team projects. Other suggestions that will help them learn more about the importance of teamwork and ergonomics include:

- Invite a communications instructor from your school to discuss effective team building strategies.
- Invite an executive from a local business to discuss the importance of the office professional and supervisor team.
- Invite an office professional from the local chapter of IAAP to discuss the importance of office layout and safety and health issues.

KEY TO SUPPLEMENTAL EXERCISE

An additional office assignment is provided in the Applications Workbook. The student is given a situation and asked to write a memorandum to Mr. Menendez offering suggestions on how the situation should be handled. The student is to use the memorandum form provided on the student template disk. Although memorandums will vary, here is a suggested solution.

TO: Juan Menendez
FROM: Student's name
DATE: Current
SUBJECT: Employee Concern

Thank you for informing me of Mao Chanren's concerns with the communications team. I was surprised; I had not observed any problems in the team. Mao always is very courteous to everyone. She does come to all meetings; however, she talks very little in the meetings. She does seem to listen and observe what is happening. I did not understand why she did not have her report, but I did not push her, believing that she would be more communicative as she felt more a part of the team.

Here is what I plan to do.

- I will set up a meeting immediately with Mao and discuss how important her membership on the team is and try to get some of her ideas about how the team should work.
- I will attempt to learn more about the Chinese culture by talking with Mr. Huang. As you know, he has been with the company for ten years; and I have worked with him on various projects. He and I have a good relationship.
- I will be very observant in regard to Mao's reactions in the meetings and outside the meetings. I will refrain from asking her for any other written reports until I know that she is comfortable with participating in this way.
- I will report to you on the progress or lack of progress that I see.

If you receive any more information from Mao, I would appreciate knowing about it. Thanks for keeping the lines of communication open.

KEY TO OFFICE PROCEDURES REINFORCEMENT

1. Define team; list and explain the standard types of internal teams that exist in an office.

    A team is a group of individuals who work together to achieve defined goals. To be effective, the team must understand and accept each other, work productively together, and consistently achieve the goals established.

    Project team—The project team works together to achieve a defined segment of work. Project teams are usually temporary in nature; when the work is accomplished, the team is dissolved.

    The office professional and the supervisor team—The effectiveness of this team depends upon mutual respect and consideration from both individuals involved.

    The office professional and coworker team—The office professional works as a team with various coworkers within the organization. In order for this team to be effective there must be acceptance, cooperation, and fairness among the individuals.

    The external team—This team is composed of individuals within the company and individuals outside the company. The external team can be part of an outsourcing endeavor of the company, special contractors with which the company works, or even customers of the company.

2. Describe your obligations as an office professional to your supervisor.
    - Acceptance. Accept your employer and avoid letting personality differences interfere with your relationship. Do not categorize your employer because of gender, age, race, or any other single characteristic.
    - Respect. Show respect for your employer's decision-making role even though you may not always understand or agree with the decisions made.
    - Loyalty. Keep confidential information confidential. Do not circumvent the chain of command; never surprise your employer.
    - Dependability. Observe the company rules.
    - Honesty. Do not take office supplies home. Do not use the telephone excessively for personal calls. Do not play games on the computer; do not access the Internet for personal use.
    - Personality traits—Adjust to your employer's work style.

3. Explain the difference between three kinds of communication: downward, upward, and horizontal.
    - Downward communication consists of messages that flow from management to the employees of the company.
    - Upward communications are messages that travel from the employees to management.

- Horizontal communication involves messages that flow from coworker to coworker or from manager to manager.

4. Define ergonomics; give three ways that ergonomics impacts the office professional.

   Ergonomics means the bringing together of the physiological factors that make an effective work environment and the psychological factors that explain how workers react to their environment. There are numerous ergonomic factors that affect employees, some of which are: color, lighting, acoustics, floor plans, and furniture and equipment.

5. Identify and explain three types of health issues that may affect the office professional. The student may list any three of the following:

   - Carpal tunnel syndrome. This syndrome is a condition that occurs due to the compression of a large nerve, the median nerve, as it passes through a tunnel composed of bone and ligaments in the wrist. Symptoms include a gradual onset of numbness and tingling or burning in the thumb and fingers.
   - Eyestrain. Symptoms of eyestrain include visual discomfort, irritation, problems in focusing, blurring, double vision, and headaches.
   - Fatigue. Sitting at a VDT for long periods of time without breaks can cause fatigue.
   - Smoking. Studies have shown that breathing secondhand smoke is unhealthy and that emphysema and lung disease are linked to secondhand smoke.
   - Substance abuse. Substance abuse refers to the use of alcohol or drugs to the extent that it is debilitating for the individual using the substance. The result of substance abuse in the office is higher absenteeism and illness.

KEY TO CRITICAL THINKING ACTIVITY

The student is given a situation and asked to respond to the questions below. Although the answers will vary, here are some possible responses.

1. Should Ben request to be taken off the team? Why or why not? Ben should not ask to be taken off the team at this point. He has no direct experience with Jennifer; all of his information is from other people. He needs to discover if it is possible for him to work with Jennifer.

2. Should Ben talk with others on the team about his concerns? Why or why not? Not at this point. Again, his information is secondhand. He should not be spreading rumors about a coworker.

3. Should Ben talk with Jennifer's supervisor? Why or why not? It is not appropriate to go to Jennifer's supervisor. If Ben does have problems with Jennifer, he should talk with her first.

4. Should Ben say nothing and concentrate on being an effective team member? Why or why not? He should say noth-

ing at this point. If problems do occur, he should go to Jennifer directly and talk with her. If the situation becomes intolerable for him as a team member (assuming that he is being open-minded and willing to listen to new information), he has the option of getting off the team. However, he needs to have real reasons for doing so, and he needs to try to work out any problems before he requests to be released from the team assignment.

KEY TO OFFICE APPLICATIONS

OA2-1 (Goal 1)

The student is to work with four classmates on this project. The project is as follows.

The local chamber of commerce has asked you to write a two-page description of your college. The chamber will be using this description in a publication they are putting together for new companies and individuals moving into the city. You need to include a short history of the college, the number of students enrolled, and the types of programs that are offered.

The group is to complete the project. In addition, they are to process how they worked as a team by answering these questions.

- What were the team's strengths?
- What problems did the team have?
- Was there expertise that the team lacked?
- If so, how did the team compensate for this lack of expertise?

The team is to write a joint memo to you (using the memorandum form in file OA02-1b), detailing how the process worked—the strengths of the team and any deficiencies the team had, listing how these deficiencies were handled. They are also to fill out a team evaluation form (OA02-1a), but it should not be submitted to you unless you request it.

OA2-2 (Goal 2)

The student is given a situation that was not handled well and asked how it could have been handled better. Although each response can differ, here is a suggested response.

How could you have handled the situation differently?

- You could have told the person that your employer was leaving for a very important professional trip and was not available, but that Ms. Adams, who is in charge while he is gone and very knowledgeable about the company, would be glad to assist her. And, then immediately walk the individual to the person's office, without giving her any time to object. Certainly, she still may have refused to see the person and stormed into your employer's office without your being able to stop her. If so, you should explain the situation to your employer. Clearly, there will be some people you cannot control regardless of what you do.

He should not blame you for these situations. However, if you are using good human relations techniques, there should be very few situations that get out of control.

What should you say to your employer, and when should you say it?

- Since he is leaving for a trip and is feeling pressured, now is not the time to get into a long discussion. Merely tell him that you are sorry that it happened and that you did attempt to get her routed to someone else. If he still seems angry, you might want to discuss with him (when he returns from his trip and has some time when the pressure is lessened) how you will handle problem situations in the future. You also should be open to any suggestions that he has.

OA2-3 (Goal 3)

The student is given a situation and asked how it should be handled. The answers will vary; here are suggested responses.

- You are not Charlotte's supervisor; you are Angelo's. You should ask Charlotte tactfully if she has talked with Angelo. If she has not, you should ask her to do so immediately. Explain that the company philosophy is one of keeping all lines of communication open and respecting the rights of the immediate supervisor. If she still insists that she must talk, listen but do not get into trying to solve the problem. Again, tell her that she needs to go to Angelo directly.

- You should tell Angelo that Charlotte came to see you. Explain how you handled the situation and be certain that he understands that if there is a problem, he needs to handle it.
- Since you have heard nothing of communication problems in the area previously, do not be accusatory with Angelo. However, you might have a discussion with him about whether he believes his socializing with employees after hours is impacting the way he treats employees. Be very clear with him that his personal life is his own business, but that his personal life and business life should not mix.
- At this point, no suggestions should be made to Angelo concerning improving communications. You do not know that there are communication problems. What you can do is ask Angelo how he thinks his team is working and if he believes there are any problems in the area. Be certain that he knows that you are supportive of him and want him to be open with you if there are problems that need to be handled.

OA2-4 (Goal 3)

The student is to key an article (from the Applications Workbook) in correct format.

The student is also to present the organization chart in an attractive and creative format.

Here is the article; the organization chart format will vary.

ON BETTER COMMUNICATIONS

Cecilia Ivon and Hugh Minor

The effectiveness of your life is determined by the effectiveness of your communication skills.

This adage sounds simple, but it is so true. Companies fail, relationships end, and sales are lost because people do not—or cannot—communicate effectively. We must routinely and consistently share our thoughts with each other so that we eliminate any confusion or misunderstanding.

Question: Are the best communicators the best talkers?

The answer is No! The best communicators are those who listen attentively. Too often hearing is confused with listening. Hearing involves detecting sound vibrations; listening means making sense from what we hear. Listening requires paying attention, interpreting what we hear, and remembering important facts.

We need to consider effective communication skills both internally and externally. We communicate internally with our fellow team members. Externally we communicate with our customers, vendors, and the general public. Our goal is to improve communications in both areas.

In communicating, there are words that negatively impact our message. Some of these words and phrases are listed below.

1. That's not my job (or department)
2. Can't
3. But
4. It's policy
5. Problem

Likewise, there are words that have a positive effect on a message. Some of these words are listed here.

1. I appreciate
2. Please
3. Opportunity
4. Thank you
5. How can I help?

People like to be around people who openly communicate and who are sincerely interested in what they are saying. Good communicators are people oriented. It takes hard work and practice to be a good communicator—but we owe it to ourselves and our customers.

By using the inverted pyramid philosophy (Figure 1) and placing the customer at the top of the organization, employees become empowered and supported by their managers to do their absolute best in communicating internally and externally.

Figure 1

OA2-5 (Goal 4)

The student is to select one of these topics to research: Ergonomics, or safety and/or health issues within the office. The student is to use three current periodicals, prepare a summary of the articles and list the references. The report is to be submitted orally to the class. The student is to prepare a memorandum to you, using the form in file OA02-5, explaining why the particular topic was chosen and how the student might use the information received in his or her present job or in a future job.

KEY TO ONLINE RESEARCH APPLICATIONS

ORA2-1 (Goals 1 and 3)

The student is to assume that he or she is giving a presentation to the local chapter of IAAP on effective communication. Using the Internet, the student is to locate at least four articles on two of the topics given below. A summary of the articles is to be prepared, listing the sources and including the URL. The summary is to be submitted to you.

Effective office communications
Building effective office teams
Listening skills
Critical thinking skills

ORA2-2 (Goal 4)

The student is to search the Internet for information on the latest office furniture available and write a short summary of the findings. The report is to be submitted to you.

CHAPTER 3

PRODUCTIVITY IN THE OFFICE

This chapter will help the student learn how to manage stress and become a productive, healthy employee. Techniques for coping with stress are presented. Since one of the major techniques for helping one to cope with multiple pressures is the ability to manage time well, time management techniques and systems are discussed in detail.

STUDENT GOALS

1. Determine why managing stress and time is important in the workplace.
2. Apply appropriate coping techniques to minimize negative stress.
3. Establish time and stress management action plans.

CHAPTER OUTLINE

I. Introduction
II. Your Goals
III. The Office Professional and Stress
   A. Stress Defined
   B. Types of Negative Stress
      1. Acute Stress
      2. Chronic Stress
   C. Cost of Stress
      1. To the Organization
      2. To the Individual
   D. Contributing Factors
      1. Role Ambiguity
      2. Job Insecurity
      3. Working Conditions and Relationships
      4. Dual-Career Families, Single Parents, and Extended Families
      5. Economic Pressures
   E. Stress Coping Techniques
      1. Do a Stress Audit
      2. Maintain a Proper Diet
      3. Set Up an Exercise Program
      4. Get the Proper Amount of Sleep
      5. Use Visualization
      6. Clarify Values
      7. Reduce Organizational Dependency
      8. Understand Role Relationships

IV. Time Management
   A. Time—A Resource
   B. Time Wasters
      1. Socializing
      2. Disorganization
      3. Ineffective Communication
      4. Procrastination
   C. Time Inventory
      1. Time Log Preparation
      2. Log Analysis
      3. Action Plan
V. Time Management Techniques
   A. Set Priorities
   B. Prepare Daily To-Do Lists
   C. Use Slack Time
   D. Handle Paperwork as Few Times as Possible
   E. Simplify Repetitive Work
   F. Perform Work Correctly the First Time
   G. Develop a Procedures Book
   H. Organize Your Workstation and Your Reading
      1. Your Desk
      2. Your Supplies
      3. Your Work Area
      4. Your Reading
   I. Use Good Communication Techniques
VI. Time Management Systems
   A. Manual Systems
      1. Calendars
      2. Tickler Files
   B. Electronic Systems
      1. Calendaring and Scheduling Meetings
      2. Emailing and Faxing
      3. Tracking Notes and Tasks
      4. Accessing Data
      5. Storing Contact Information
VII. Summary
VIII. Key Terms
IX. Professional Pointers
X. Office Procedures Reinforcement
XI. Critical Thinking Activity
XII. Office Applications
XIII. Online Research Applications

TEACHING SUGGESTIONS

- Invite a nutritionist to your class to discuss proper diet.
- If you have an exercise facility on your campus, make arrangements with the instructor to go through several stress reduction exercises with your entire class, with the class as active participants.
- Ask class members to attempt to work three hours of exercise into their activities for the next three weeks; at the completion of the three weeks, ask class members to give an oral report on whether or not the exercise reduced some of the stress in their lives.

KEY TO SUPPLEMENTAL EXERCISE

The student is given a case and asked to respond to the three items listed below. The student is asked to share his or her responses in small group discussions with class members. Responses will vary; suggested responses are given here.

1. Describe what may result if Chang continues to handle his situation as he currently does.

   He probably will not be able to finish the major project on time, which could mean a poor evaluation or even loss of his job. There is a good possibility that Chang will become physically sick due to the constant workload. He already is feeling emotionally "burned out." The result of his physical and emotional stress for the company may be lack of productivity and increase in sick leave, both of which will cost the company money.

2. How can Chang manage his time more efficiently?

   He should set aside a certain period of uninterrupted time each day when he works on the project; it is imperative that he "catch up" and complete the project on the due date. He should seek assistance in addressing the computer system problems that are occurring in the office. If there is no one available in the company, he may contact an outside firm to provide a qualified person for the job. He should take his lunch hours. If he does not, he probably will feel more stress and be less productive. It probably is a good idea to postpone his vacation for two months, until the project is completed.

3. Does he need to talk with his supervisor about the situation? If so, what does he say to her?

   Yes, he should talk with his supervisor. He should explain to her that he is not able to keep up with the additional workload brought about by the new computer system and finish the major project also. He should present her with a plan for solving the problem; i.e., additional help to work on the computer problems.

KEY TO OFFICE PROCEDURES REINFORCEMENT

1. Explain why the workplace can be stressful and the difference between negative stress (including acute and chronic stress) and positive stress.

   Numerous factors contribute to workplace stress, some of which are:

   - Role ambiguity
   - Job insecurity
   - Working conditions and relationships
   - Work overload
   - Personal problems
   - Dual-career families and single parents
   - Economic pressures

   Stress is the response of the body to a demand made upon it. Positive stress causes us to satisfy our goals. Negative stress, referred to as distress, results when the stress in our lives has a negative effect on us; for example a negative performance review. Acute stress occurs when a person has to respond instantaneously to a crisis situation. Chronic stress occurs when a distressful situation is prolonged with no rest or recuperation for the body.

2. List and explain five strategies that will help you cope with stress.

   The student may list any five of the following:

   - Do a stress audit. Make a list of the circumstances that contribute to your negative stress. Ask yourself which of the circumstances you can do something about. Prepare a plan of action detailing what you plan to do.
   - Maintain a proper diet. Lower the intake of fat, sugar, salt, and caffeine in your diet. Be sure that your diet is rich in fruits, vegetables, cereals, and legumes.
   - Set up an exercise program. Determine a regular time of day that you will exercise and then begin a program that you enjoy. Be consistent with the program each week.
   - Get the proper amount of sleep. Studies have shown that people who sleep seven to eight hours a night tend to live longer than people whose sleep is longer or shorter. If you have trouble going to sleep, practice techniques (such as taking a hot bath, reading before going to bed, and so forth) that will help you.
   - Use visualization. Visualization helps you block out unwanted thoughts that can cause stress. When using visualization, you must get into a comfortable position, relax any muscles that feel tense, and begin to visualize a pleasant scene.
   - Clarify values. Values are principles that guide your life, such as honesty, fairness, love, and so forth. Take time to assess your values. Ask yourself if you live these values in your daily life. Consistently paying attention to your

values and being committed to living them daily will reduce significantly the negative stress that you face.

- Reduce organizational dependency. Educate and train
  yourself to be employable by a number of companies.
- Understand role relationships. Be sensitive to the needs
  of your employer and your coworkers. Know what they
  expect of you. Know how you fit into the organizational
  structure.

3. Define time and explain four time wasters.

Time is a resource that cannot be bought, sold, rented, borrowed, saved, or manufactured. We spend it, even if we accomplish nothing.

Time wasters include:

- Socializing
- Disorganization
- Ineffective communication
- Procrastination

4. List and explain five time management techniques.

The student may list and explain any five of the following:

- Set priorities.
- Prepare daily to-do lists.
- Use slack time.
- Handle paperwork as few times as possible.
- Simplify repetitive work.
- Perform work correctly the first time.
- Develop a procedures book.
- Organize your workstation and your reading.
- Use good communication techniques.

5. Describe how PIM software can help you manage your
   time.

PIM software allows you to organize your work quickly
and efficiently. It allows you to:

- Calendar and schedule meetings
- Email and fax
- Track notes and tasks
- Access data
- Store contact information

KEY TO CRITICAL THINKING ACTIVITY

The student is given a case and asked to respond to these
items:

1. Describe the factors that contribute to the stress Beverly is
   feeling.

- New job
- Required to use spreadsheet software and has not used it
  previously

- Must supervise two office professionals; has never supervised employees
- Demanding, workaholic boss

2. What steps can she take to help her cope with the stress?

- Read her job description carefully; be clear about her
  role.
- Make a list of the things that are causing her stress; then
  do an action plan to address these issues.
- Maintain a proper diet.
- Exercise weekly.
- Get the proper amount of sleep.

3. If you were Beverly, how would you attempt to get control
   of the job?

- Give yourself time to learn the job; accept that you will
  make some mistakes initially.
- Ask a coworker for help with the spreadsheet software if
  you do not understand certain portions.
- Read current literature on supervision of employees;
  practice good human relations skills with the employees;
  allow yourself time to learn how to supervise; let the employees know that you have much to learn and that you
  hope you can learn together.
- Accept Mr. Evans' work habits; do not judge him.

KEY TO OFFICE APPLICATIONS

OA3-1 (Goal 1)

If the student is working presently, the student is to interview
his or her supervisor concerning stress and time management,
asking these questions:

1. Is stress a problem in the workplace? If so, how do the employees in the company exhibit stress?
2. What is the cost of stress to the company?
3. Does the company offer any workshops or seminars for
   employees in handling stress and managing time appropriately?
4. Do you have suggestions for helping employees deal with
   stress and manage time?

The student is to write a short report of the interview and
present the report orally to the class. A written report is to be
submitted to you, giving the name and company of the person
interviewed.

If the student is not working presently, he or she is to read
two recent articles (within the last two years) on the cost of
stress to companies and time management techniques. A short
summary is to be written of the articles, noting the sources.
The report is to be submitted orally to the class and in writing
to you.

OA3-2 (Goals 2 and 3)

The student is to complete the Stress Audit given in the Applications Workbook, pages 15–18. After completing the Stress Audit, the student is to prepare an action plan, listing steps to take in an attempt to reduce stress. The Action Plan form is given on the student template disk in file OA03-2. The items are not to be submitted to you. The student is to keep the Stress Audit and at the end of the course, retake it to determine if he or she has been able to reduce stress.

OA3-3 (Goal 2)

Using the student template disk, file OA03-3a, the student is to prioritize the items. Using the student template disk, file OA03-3b, the student is to read the email message and then reclassify the priorities on the to-do list. A short paragraph is to be written justifying the realignment of the priorities. A copy is to be submitted to you.

First Priorities Established

Arrange an interview within the next week for Mr. Menendez.
Meet the France Vice President at the airport at 2 p.m.
Submit professional development plan due at end of week.
Schedule next month's planning conference.
Distribute monthly newsletter.
Order computer supplies.
Update performance goals for annual evaluation.
File correspondence for the last week.
Purge computer files.

Reevaluation of Priorities

Arrange trip for Mr. Menendez.
Call the business manager for the income and expense figures.
   Meet the France Vice President at the airport at 2 p.m.
   Submit professional development plan due at end of week.
   Schedule next month's planning conference.
   Distribute monthly newsletter.
   Order computer supplies.
   Update performance goals for annual evaluation.
   File correspondence for the last week.
   Purge computer files.

Since Mr. Menendez must go to Frankfurt next week, the reservations must be made immediately. I will start the arrangements in the morning. If I cannot finish before picking up the France VP at 2 p.m., I will finish them later in the afternoon. The business manager also needs to be called in the morning early so that he can have enough time to get the income and expense figures to Mr. Menendez by tomorrow.

OA3-4 (Goal 3)

Using the Daily Time Logs provided on pages 19–21 of the Applications Workbook, the student is to log the time spent in various activities for the next five days. If the student is employed, he or she is to log the time spent in activities at work. If not, he or she is to log the use of personal time. Then the student is to answer the questions on the Time Management Analysis on page 23 of the Applications Workbook. Using the Action Plan form on the student template disk in file OA03-4, the student is to prepare an action plan. The plan is to be submitted to you.

KEY TO ONLINE RESEARCH APPLICATIONS

ORA3-5 (Goal 1)

Using the Internet, the student is to research the following topics:

- Stress coping techniques
- Time management techniques

The student is to summarize two recent articles (within the past two years) from the search. The summary is to be submitted to you, with the sources listed.

ORA3-6 (Goal 2)

Using the Internet, the student is to research the cost of stress to business. The research is to be presented orally to the class.

CHAPTER 4

ETHICAL BEHAVIOR

In this chapter, ethics is considered a pragmatic topic that is to be understood conceptually and practiced in the day-to-day operation of a business and in the lives of employees within the business. The chapter provides the student a framework that allows for the understanding of the importance of ethics and the characteristics of ethical organizations. The chapter also provides practical suggestions for the office professional on behaving ethically.

STUDENT GOALS

1. Explain the importance of ethical behavior in the workplace.
2. Identify the characteristics of an ethical organization.
3. Identify the characteristics of an ethical office professional.
4. Determine how to achieve ethical change.

CHAPTER OUTLINE

I. Introduction
II. Your Goals
III. Business Ethics
   A. A Historical Evolution of Business Ethics
   B. The Why
   C. The How
IV. The Ethical Organization
   A. Environmentally Responsible
   B. Internationally Aware
   C. Culturally Committed to Behaving Ethically
   D. Honest
   E. Committed to Diversity
   F. Committed to the Community
   G. Committed to Employees
   H. An Establisher of Standards
V. Ethical Change
   A. Factors Impeding Ethical Change
      1. Values cannot be changed
      2. Organizations are amoral
      3. Labels accurately describe individuals
      4. The leadership of an organization never behaves ethically
   B. Steps Producing Ethical Change
      1. Determine the ethical change required
      2. Determine the steps required to achieve the objective

3. Practice the new behaviors
4. Seek feedback
5. Reward the group and individuals involved
6. Evaluate the effects of the ethical change
VI. Discrimination
   A. Sexual Harassment
   B. Racial Discrimination
VII. Characteristics of the Ethical Office Professional
   A. Makes Ethical Decisions
   B. Supports Ethical Behavior
   C. Refuses to Engage in Negative Office Politics
   D. Accepts Constructive Criticism
   E. Observes Office Hours
   F. Accepts Responsibilities
   G. Maintains Honesty and Integrity
   H. Respects Privacy
   I. Is Open to Change
   J. Is Loyal
   K. Keeps the Faith
VIII. Summary
   IX. Key Terms
   X. Professional Pointers
   XI. Office Procedures Reinforcement
   XII. Critical Thinking Activity
   XIII. Office Applications
   XIV. Online Research Applications

TEACHING SUGGESTIONS

- Invite business representatives to discuss with the class ethical situations within the business and how these situations were handled.
- Have students discuss as a group how their early childhood training and experiences have influenced their values.
- Ask the students to interview office professionals concerning an ethical problem they have had and how they solved the problem.
- Stress to students as you begin this chapter and as they read and complete the assignments that:
   —They are not to judge others who have a different point of view than their own.
   —They are to listen to others and attempt to understand their way of looking at situations, especially if it is different than their own.
   —They will have their own opinions and biases but should not attempt to force them on other people.

- Commit (as the instructor) to being open-minded to students, listening to them, and helping them understand how to evaluate situations based on their own values—not your value system.
- Peruse the DePaul University Institute for Business and Professional Ethics Web site (http://condor.depaul.edu/ethics/resource.html) for ideas and resources.

KEY TO SUPPLEMENTAL EXERCISES

There are two supplemental exercises given in this chapter.

Supplemental Exercise 1

The student is given an ethical exercise in the Applications Workbook consisting of seven statements to read and decide whether or not he or she agrees or disagrees with each statement. After the form is completed, the student is to discuss the answers with his or her classmates in groups of three or four.

Supplemental Exercise 2

The students are to work in teams of three or four to develop a Credo for a company where they would like to work; they may use the Johnson & Johnson Credo as a resource as they develop their own. Once the Credo has been developed, they are to key it in an attractive format, using graphics.

KEY TO OFFICE PROCEDURES REINFORCEMENT

1. List and explain six characteristics of an ethical organization.

   The student may list and explain any six of the following characteristics:

   - Environmentally responsible
   - Internationally aware
   - Culturally committed to behaving ethically
   - Honest
   - Committed to diversity
   - Committed to the community
   - Committed to employees
   - An establisher of standards

2. Explain three factors that impede ethical change.

   The student may explain any three of the following factors:

   - Values cannot be changed.
   - Organizations are amoral.
   - Labels accurately describe individuals.
   - The leadership of an organization never behaves ethically.

3. How can ethical change be encouraged within an organization? Discuss a minimum of five steps that can be taken in encouraging ethical change.

The student may discuss any five of the following steps:

- Determine the ethical change required.
- Determine the steps required to achieve the objective.
- Practice the new behaviors.
- Seek feedback.
- Reward the group and individuals involved.
- Evaluate the effects of the ethical change.

4. List five steps you can take if you are a victim of sexual harassment or racial discrimination.

   The student may list any five of the following steps:

   - Know your rights.
   - Keep a record of all sexual harassment and racial discrimination infractions, noting the dates, incidents, and witnesses (if any).
   - File a formal grievance with the company.
   - If your employer is not responsive to your complaint, file charges of discrimination with the federal and state agencies that enforce civil rights laws, such as the EEOC.
   - Talk to friends, coworkers, and relatives. It is important to avoid isolation and self-blame.
   - Consult an attorney to investigate legal alternatives to discriminatory or sexual harassment behaviors.

5 Explain five characteristics of an ethical office professional.

   The student may list any five of the following characteristics:

   - Makes ethical decisions
   - Supports ethical behavior
   - Refuses to engage in negative office politics
   - Accepts constructive criticism
   - Observes office hours
   - Accepts responsibilities
   - Maintains honesty and integrity
   - Respects privacy
   - Is open to change
   - Is loyal
   - Keeps the faith

KEY TO CRITICAL THINKING ACTIVITY

The student is given a case and asked to answer the following questions. Although answers will vary, suggested responses are given.

- Should Ahmed ignore the behavior of his colleagues or express his concern? If so, to whom?

   Ahmed should not ignore the behavior of his colleagues since he finds the behavior offensive. He should not grandstand about the issue or make hurtful remarks to anyone in the group. Rather, Ahmed should quietly and tactfully say to the coordinator that he is uncomfortable hearing ethnically biased jokes. He can say to the group that he considers the jokes offensive, or he can make an obvious statement by walking away from the group when they are telling stories that are offensive.

- Should Ahmed express concern about the behavior of the coordinator? If so, to whom?

  As indicated in the previous answer, he should express concern first to the coordinator. If the offensive behavior continues, he may want to say something to the person to whom the coordinator reports. Such action is risky; Ahmed may experience some negative reaction as a result, even the loss of a future job. However, standing up for his values may be more important to Ahmed than compromising them for a job. If Ahmed compromises this time, he may find himself compromising on other values. If this company is going to support the offensive behavior, it probably is best to move to another company.

- Will Ahmed jeopardize his opportunity in the management trainee program if he complains about the coordinator's behavior?

  Although he should not jeopardize his opportunity, he may. Ahmed is face-to-face with a very real value dilemma. What is more important—his values or the job? The answer is a tough one, but one many people encounter at some point in their careers.

KEY TO OFFICE APPLICATIONS

OA4-1 (Goals 1, 2, and 4)

The student is to work with two classmates on this activity. They are to read two recent articles (within the last two years) on the importance of ethical behavior in the workplace and how individuals can be helped to behave ethically. From their research, they are to analyze how the behaviors advocated affect the workplace. They are to consider how ethical behaviors impact management, employees, and customers. They are also to make several suggestions for achieving ethical change within an organization. The findings are to be compiled in a report of no more than four pages and submitted to you.

OA4-2 (Goal 2)

The student is given a case and asked to work with two or three classmates on the responses. The students' suggestions are to be given in an oral report to the class.

The students are asked to answer these questions. Answers will vary; given below are suggested responses.

- What decision should be made in this case?

  Pull the drug from the market immediately and notify the press of its possible effects; continue the research on the drug. The administration should also notify the auditors that there are potential problems that may have negative financial impact.

- Give reasons for making the decision.

  Six people who have been taking the drug have died; it is not clear whether or not the drug caused the deaths. Additional deaths may occur. In addition to the ethical problems, there are also legal problems (the probability of lawsuits) with the deaths that have already occurred and increased exposure to litigation if there are more deaths. The auditors must be told of any circumstances that may cause negative financial impact. Not to disclose this information, and to sign a statement that there are none, is dishonest.

Each individual team member is to determine whether or not the decision made by the group is considered an ethical one by the individual. The student is to justify his or her response by explaining how the decision is or is not ethical. Then the student is to explain how his or her own ethics impacted the person's individual decision. (In other words, the student may have disagreed with the team's discussion but was not able to convince the team that the decision was wrong.)

OA4-3 (Goals 2 and 3)

The student is given four cases and asked to work with three classmates on answering the questions given at the end of the cases. A short report of the answers is to be prepared and submitted to the instructor. Answers will vary; suggested responses are given.

Case 1

- Is it ethical to take advantage of this offer? If so, why? If not, why not?

  It is not a good idea to take advantage of the offer. It could be considered as a payment for your selection of the hotel; in that case, it is unethical. It could be merely a marketing tool for the company. However, your affirmative response to the offer still would be questionable. It is much better not to accept any "perks" from the hotel. This situation is one that you would not want to see the next day in the paper reported as "Employee accepts bribes from company in exchange for business."

Case 2

- Was his behavior ethical or unethical? Justify your answers.

  Since the discount coupon was not tied to any specific favors Dave had performed for the company, his behavior is not unethical. However, it is questionable. Even if the software vendor does no business with the company at the present time, it may do so in the future. Dave may have the opportunity to recommend a software vendor at some point. If he recommended the company (even though its product was the best for the situation), he is suspect due to his past behavior.

- Was the company justified in firing him? Why or why not?

Firing is probably not justified, knowing that he has not been working for the company for long and that there has been no code of conduct given to Dave that he has been expected to uphold. However, he should be told that any future conduct such as the acceptance of gifts or favors will have serious repercussions. If the company does not have a value statement and does not make employees aware of a code of conduct to follow, it should develop one.

Case 3

- Should Susan let her boss know that she feels there is a double standard? Or should she keep quiet?

It depends on how strongly Susan feels about the situation. There does seem to be a double standard; however, if there are no other practices that Susan objects to, it is probably not important enough to call attention to it. If she does say something to her boss, she should approach it by telling him that she does not understand why the company has a rule against gifts being accepted by employees, yet the executives accept gifts from a vendor. She could ask him to help her understand how the rule is implemented.

Case 4

- What advice would you give your coworker?

She should write down the situation exactly as it happened, noting the date and time. She should keep the written document in a locked location where no one has access to it; she might choose to keep it at home. If her employer approaches her again, she should let him know that she finds his suggestion extremely offensive and considers it harassment. She should then report the situation to the Human Resource Officer of the company.

KEY TO ONLINE RESEARCH APPLICATIONS

ORA4-4 (Goal 1)

The student is to search the Web for articles about companies who have lived their values through specific incidences. The student is to attempt to find three stories of companies. A copy of the stories is to be made and submitted to the instructor, with an oral report to the class.

ORA4-5 (Goals 2 and 4)

The student is to select three classmates to work with on this project. The student is to search for vision/value statements for three companies. Copies of the statements are to be printed out. As a team, a short summary (approximately two pages) is to be written, listing the company names and giving a critique of the statements. These questions are to be answered:

- Are the statements clear?
- Do they spell out sufficiently the values by which the company will operate?

- Will they inspire support from employees?
- If you were a manager in charge of helping employees who report to you live the values espoused by these statements within the business, how would you go about doing it?

The students are to report orally to the class on their findings or submit a report in writing to you.

KEY TO END OF PART 1 ACTIVITIES

Vocabulary Review: Part 1 (Chapters 1–4)

1. virtual environment
2. continuous quality improvement or total quality management
3. job sharing
4. critical thinking
5. creativity
6. values
7. tact
8. outsourcing
9. horizontal communication
10. ergonomics
11. stress
12. chronic stress
13. role ambiguity
14. downsizing
15. time
16. tickler file
17. ethics
18. moral integrity
19. organizational culture
20. stereotyping
21. prejudice
22. amoral
23. quid pro quo
24. bias
25. social responsibility

Language Skills Practice: Part 1 (Chapters 1–4)

1. Elizabeth H. Crowther, Ph.D., is teaching an organizational behavior course during the spring semester.
2. Dr. Josef Landow, Mr. Harry Curns, and Mrs. Angelis Franz make up the law firm of Landow, Curns, and Franz.
3. Carl Sandburg is my favorite poet; he wrote these lines: Why did he write to her, "I can't live with you"? And why did she write to him, "I can't live without you"? For he went west, she went east, And they both lived.
4. He plans to take algebra in the fall and psychology in the spring.

5. Next semester Sharon and Carlos will enroll in Ethics 212.

6. Every visitor to Italy will want to see three of the wonders of the ancient world.

7. In the twenty-first century there will be major changes in the international economy.

8. The director will be away for an hour.

9. We will gladly accept your offer.

10. Net profit has dropped except during 1994.

11. We will leave the house about ten o'clock.

12. Marcus, Monique, and Harlan were second, third, and fourth runners-up in the extemporaneous speaking contest.

13. Fulton-Calkins's book was published by South-Western Educational Publishing, an International Thomson Publishing Company.

14. Does this price, Ms. Holzback, include both the building and equipment?

15. The professor spoke with authority; that is, she set down the rules and expected them to be observed.

16. Jan, Mary, and June attended the meeting today; Mark and Todd attended the meeting yesterday.

17. The company has increased its volume of business by nearly 200 percent over the past year—no small achievement in these times.

18. Neither Heather nor Kevin plans to attend the communications seminar.

19. Beginning this week, our office will be located at One Main Place.

20. items
    Rule: Do not divide words of five or fewer letters.

21. months
    Rule: Do not divide one-syllable words.

22. neces-sary
    Rule: Divide between double consonants that appear within a word.

PART 2: OFFICE TECHNOLOGY

CHAPTER 5

INFORMATION PROCESSING

To say that our world is a computerized one is a cliché. The computer has changed not only the way we work, but the way we live and our expectations of service. The twenty-first century promises to bring additional technological advances that will impact the way we work, learn, play, and interact with each other. The office professional must have an understanding of computer directions and a willingness to continue to learn. This chapter is an overview of computer hardware and systems.

STUDENT GOALS

1. Identify methods of creating and inputting information.
2. Define and use storage devices.
3. Output information.
4. Identify projected future computer directions.

CHAPTER OUTLINE

I. Introduction
II. Your Goals
III. Information Creation
IV. Information Input
   A. Computer Keyboards
   B. Scanners
      1. OCR (Optical Character Reader) Scanners
      2. MICR (Magnetic Ink Character Readers)
      3. Barcode Scanners
      4. Handheld Scanners
   C. Speech/Voice-Recognition Technology
   D. Mice and Trackballs
   E. Touch Screens
   F. Touch Pads
   G. Infrared Devices
   H. Pen Tablets and Pucks

V. Information Processing
   A. Computer Classifications
      1. Supercomputers
      2. Mainframe Computers
      3. Minicomputers
      4. Workstation Computers (Supermicros)
      5. Microcomputers (Personal Computers)
   B. Computer Internal Processing and Storage
      1. Central Processing Unit
      2. Arithmetic/Logic Unit
      3. Control Unit
      4. Memory
   C. Storage Devices
      1. Floppy Disks
      2. Zip Disks and Drives
      3. Compact Disc Storage
      4. Hard Disks
      5. Magnetic Tape
VI. Information Output
   A. Monitors
   B. Image Quality and Size
   C. Printers
      1. Inkjets
      2. Lasers
   D. Multifunction Peripherals
   E. Networked Printers
VII. Computer Networks
   A. Internet
   B. World Wide Web
   C. Intranet
   D. Extranet
VIII. Future Directions of Computer Technology
IX. Summary
X. Key Terms
XI. Professional Pointers
XII. Office Procedures Reinforcement
XIII. Critical Thinking Activity
XIV. Office Applications
XV. Online Research Applications

TEACHING SUGGESTIONS

- Invite a manager of the computer division of a local business to talk with your students about the directions the company is taking, the issues that are facing the employees in keeping current with computer technology, and what the manager anticipates as to future directions the company will be taking.
- Have the students read (or listen to tapes) of some of the visionary thinking in the computer world. For example, you might ask students to research some of the thinking of Bill Gates of Microsoft.

KEY TO SUPPLEMENTAL EXERCISE

An additional office assignment is provided in the Applications Workbook. The student is to prepare a memorandum, using the database file entitled SE05a. Students were instructed to make several changes to the SE05a file first. The corrected file is shown below.

Name	Department	Work Phone Number	Employment Date
Ruth Adams	Communications	1-1501	10/95
Alexandria VanDern	Communications	1-1505	10/95
Richard Austin	Information Systems	1-1806	1/2000
Edmond Jones	Personnel	1-1783	1/85
Mark McGuire	Personnel	1-1893	1/87
Daphne Newsome	Communications	1-1510	8/95
Chuck McDowel	Information Systems	1-9668	6/95
Rosemary Lipstein	Communications	1-1512	3/88
Ralph Dillon	Communications	1-1522	4/87
Richard Maris	Personnel	1-1875	5/88
Ruth Billingsley	Communications	1-1500	10/95
Tokomoto Kamoda	Information Systems	1-9665	7/95

These employees are to receive a memorandum showing five years of service:

Ruth Adams
Ruth Billingsley
Tokomoto Kamoda
Daphne Newsome
Chuck McDowel
Alexandria VanDern

This employee is to receive a memorandum showing one year of service:

Richard Austin
TO: (Employee's name)
FROM: Hugh Minor
DATE: (Current)
SUBJ: Anniversary Recognition

All of us at People First International want to express our thanks to you for helping to make our company one of the best in the industry. When you joined (one/five) year(s) ago, you became a part of a winning team.

In the past year, our job placements rose by 8 percent; but even more important, our profitability improved by 10 percent. Your continued commitment to providing a quality service to our customers has contributed to this outstanding performance.

It takes the entire team to make People First International the industry leader that it is today. However, the team can be no greater than each of its capable and dedicated employees. YOU make our team what it is.

Congratulations on your (first/fifth) anniversary with us. We look forward to celebrating many successes together!

KEY TO OFFICE PROCEDURES REINFORCEMENT

1. Identify three methods of creating and inputting information.

   The student may give any three of the following.

   Creating
   - Longhand draft
   - Computer draft
   - Shorthand
   - Machine dictation

   Inputting
   - Computer keyboards
   - Scanners
   - Voice-recognition systems
   - Mice and trackballs
   - Touch screens
   - Touch pads
   - Infrared devices
   - Pen tablets and pucks

2. Define and explain the various classifications of computers.

   - Supercomputers are the largest and fastest computers in the industry. They can operate at 1.06 teraflops per second, and it is expected that their speed will increase, with 1 petaflop per second predicted by 2002.

- Mainframe computers are large computers that accommodate hundreds of users doing different tasks. They are commonly found in large businesses and government agencies. They support a number of auxiliary devices such as terminals, printers, disk drives, and other input and output equipment.
- Minicomputers are midrange computers and are generally used in middle-size business. They are slower, have less storage capacity, and are less expensive than a mainframe computer.
- Workstation computers (supermicros) are the upper-end machines of the microcomputer. They have a large amount of process power, approaching the power of a mainframe. They have a high-speed microprocessor, significantly increased memory and hard-disk storage capacity over the microcomputer, and are able to serve several users.
- Microcomputers (personal computers) are the smallest of the computer systems. Today, microcomputers are as powerful as many mainframe computers of several years ago. One relatively recent technological invention, the Pentium processor chip, has increased the speed and performance capability of the PC.

3. Define and explain four storage devices.

The student may define and explain any four of the following storage devices:

- Floppy disks
- Zip disks and drives
- Compact disks
- Hard disks
- Magnetic tapes

4. Explain how you output information.

Information may be output through:

- Monitors
- Printers
- Multifunction peripherals
- Networked printers

5. Explain the difference between the Internet and the World Wide Web.

The Internet is the world's largest group of connected computers, allowing people from all over the world to communicate. The Internet is a vehicle for delivering information back and forth between computers around the world.

The Web is a huge collection of computer files scattered across the Internet. The Web is a portion of the information available through the Internet. For example, in addition to the Web, the Internet contains news articles, weather information, entertainment, email, travel information, and encyclopedic information, to name a few.

KEY TO CRITICAL THINKING ACTIVITY

The student is given a case and asked to answer the following questions. Answers will vary; suggested responses are given.

1. What type of computer would you recommend Richard buy for the business and why?

A microcomputer is appropriate since Riverfront Properties is a small real estate firm.

2. What type of printer would you recommend Richard purchase and why?

A color laser printer is appropriate since Richard will need to produce quality brochures of property available for sale. The printer does not need to be an extremely expensive one.

3. Should Richard recommend a scanner? If so, why and what type of scanner?

Yes, a scanner would be helpful in scanning property and other types of real estate information. A flatbed scanner will be appropriate, since the office will occasionally need to scan bound copy. He should investigate a printer/scanner unit since the scanning needs will not be large.

4. Should Richard recommend voice-recognition software? Assuming that the employees are not extremely proficient on a keyboard, voice-recognition software should be recommended.

KEY TO OFFICE APPLICATIONS

OA5-1 (Goal 1)

The students are to prepare a report to be presented orally to the class. For several days, they are to observe different methods of inputting data into computer systems. They will find examples such as:

- Grocery stores where items and prices are scanned; total bills are calculated by the computers.
- Department stores where handheld scanners are used to input an item's bar code.
- Banks' automated teller machines to record deposits, make withdrawals, transfer money, get balances.
- Gas stations with automatic credit-card payment.

OA5-2 (Goals 2 and 3)

Students are given a database format on their template disk; they are to record data pertaining to computer training sessions. After the database file is established, they are to query the file and provide a schedule for each of the instructors. The schedules are as follows.

SCHEDULE FOR J. HOBSON

Session	Date	Time	Room No.
Microcomputers and DOS	11–2	8:30–12:30	21A
Advanced DOS and Software Utilities	11–5	1:30–4:30	21A
Microcomputers and DOS	11–16	8:30–12:30	21A
Microcomputers and DOS	11–20	8:30–12:30	21A
Spreadsheets, Level I	11–21	8:30–12:30	21C
Spreadsheets, Level II	11–23	1:30–4:30	21C

SCHEDULE FOR S. KAUBICS

Session	Date	Time	Room No.
Word Processing Applications	11–9	8:30–12:30	21B
Word Processing Applications	11–16	8:30–12:30	21B
Advanced OS and Software Utilities	11–16	1:30–4:30	21A

SCHEDULE FOR I. WELSH

Session	Date	Time	Room No.
Word Processing Applications	11–5	8:30–12:30	21A
Creating Macros	11–9	2:30–4:30	21B
Word Processing Applications	11–12	8:30–12:30	21A
Creating Macros	11–16	8:30–12:30	21B
Spreadsheets, Level II	11–17	1:30–4:30	21A

SCHEDULE FOR B. SERWINZT

Session	Date	Time	Room No.
Spreadsheets, Level I	11–4	8:30–12:30	21C
Introduction to Presentation Software	11–16	8:30–10:30	21A
Spreadsheets, Level I	11–17	8:30–12:30	21C
Introduction to Presentation Software	11–23	8:30–10:30	21C

OA5-3 (Goal 2 and 3)

The student is to use the same database file that was used in OA5-2 and develop a room chart, showing dates and times.

TRAINING ROOM AVAILABILITY CHART
(X indicates open)

Date	Time	Rm 21A	Rm 21B	Rm 21C
Nov. 2	8:30–12:30		X	X
Nov. 12	8:30–10:30		X	X
	1:30–4:30	X	X	X
Nov. 16	1:30–4:30			X
Nov. 20	1:30–4:30	X	X	
Nov. 21	8:30–4:30	X	X	

The student is to make a backup of the chart on a floppy disk. One copy is to be submitted to you.

OA5-4 (Goals 2 and 3)

In the Applications Workbook on pages 36–38 is a rough-draft copy of an article for the company's newsletter, authored by Paul Simmins. The student is to key the copy, making corrections as indicated, adding graphics, and formatting the document in two columns.

CONFERENCE HIGHLIGHTS
by Paul Simmins

The Century 21 Communication Network Conference held in Chicago last week would have caused even non-computer "nuts" to get excited. Billed as an innovative technology showcase, the conference unveiled networking systems, imaging capabilities, and highly sophisticated personal information manager products.

Imaging

Aldron, Inc., introduced its document imaging software, which is used to add faxed and scanned images into certain applications. The images can be copied, stored, manipulated, and distributed with applications such as electronic mail or databases.

PIM

A new PIM from Lorenz tops an outliner and database to cross-reference data stored in its calendar, phone book, and to-do-list modules. This software will be available in stand-alone and networked versions. If we were to install this software on our network, it would enable group scheduling and multiuser outlining features.

Networking Systems

I was intrigued with a networking system that may be a possibility for our satellite centers. The system permits up to 35 users to share files, printers, and other peripheral equipment. The LAN does not require technical expertise for installation, since it connects easily to each PC's parallel port.

Teleconferencing

The latest in teleconferencing was previewed by KOVANET. Network users can participate in electronic conferences regardless of their location. Security can be assured, and a feature for notetaking is built in.

User Group Reminder

At next month's user group meeting, I will provide additional information from the conference. The main topic for the meeting, however, will be how to more efficiently use the local area network for sharing files.

Make a note of questions you may have or shortcuts you would like to know. I will see you at the meeting.

KEY TO ONLINE RESEARCH APPLICATIONS

ORA5-5 (Goal 4)

The student is to use the Internet to research advances in voice recognition. A short report is to be written of the findings, identifying sources. A copy is to be submitted to you.

ORA5-6 (Goal 4)

The student is to discover, through Internet research, how computer technology is expected to impact our lives in the next five to ten years. A short report is to be written of the findings, identifying sources. A copy is to be submitted to you.

CHAPTER 6

COMPUTER SOFTWARE

The intent of this chapter is to give the student an overview of the various types of software available—not a detailed knowledge of any one package. It is expected that he or she will have taken a prior course in one or more software packages and is competent on those packages. In addition to software knowledge, the student will also learn how to select and properly care for computers and software.

STUDENT GOALS

1. Demonstrate an understanding of operating systems and applications software.
2. Troubleshoot software problems.
3. Describe how to care for hardware and software.
4. Explain how to select software.
5. Use applications software in performing tasks.

CHAPTER OUTLINE

I. Introduction
II. Your Goals
III. Software Programs
    A. Operating Systems Software
       1. DOS
       2. Windows
       3. Windows NT
       4. OS/390 and OS/400
       5. UNIX
       6. Mac OS
    B. Operating System Functions
    C. Applications Software
       1. Word Processing
       2. Bundles
       3. Integrated Software or Office Suites
       4. Graphics
       5. Spreadsheets
       6. Personal Information/Contact Managers
       7. Database Managers
       8. Voice Recognition
       9. Remote Access
      10. Presentation Software
      11. Privacy Software
      12. Internet Software
IV. Troubleshooting
V. Computer Ergonomics and Ethics
    A. Productivity and Comfort Suggestions
    B. Software Selection
    C. Software Care
    D. Security Procedures
    E. Software Copying
    F. Computer Viruses
VI. Summary
VII. Key Terms
VIII. Professional Pointers
IX. Office Procedures Reinforcement
X. Critical Thinking Activity
XI. Office Applications
XII. Online Research Application

TEACHING SUGGESTIONS

- Invite a software vendor to introduce one of the latest software packages—possibly a new voice-recognition software program.
- Invite a specialist from the college computer department to:
  a. Explain the criteria used when recommending a software package for the entire college.
  b. Offer suggestions on troubleshooting software packages. You might want to ask the students to be prepared with specific questions to ask the person concerning problems they have experienced.
  c. Explain what operating system is used by the college and why.

KEY TO SUPPLEMENTAL EXERCISE

On page 44 of the Applications Workbook, the student is given information about a company-wide software survey. The student is to create a bar graph from this information and submit it to you. Although graphs will vary, here is one example.

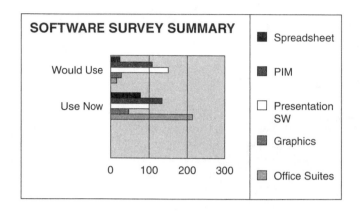

KEY TO OFFICE PROCEDURES REINFORCEMENT

1. Explain the term "operating system" and name three commonly used operating systems.

    An operating system controls the systems of your computer, keyboard, printer, mouse, and other peripheral devices. It is a program that enables your computer to read and write data to a disk, send pictures to your monitor, and accept keyboard commands.

    The student may name any three of the following:

    - DOS
    - Windows
    - Windows NT
    - OS/390 and OS/400
    - UNIX
    - Mac OS

2. Name and describe five types of applications software.

    The student may name and describe any five of the following:

    - Word processing
    - Bundles
    - Integrated software or suites
    - Graphics
    - Spreadsheets
    - PIM
    - Database managers
    - Voice recognition
    - Remote access
    - Presentation software
    - Privacy software
    - Internet software

3. Explain what troubleshooting means; list three troubleshooting helps that are available on software packages.

    Troubleshooting consists of determining the steps that you can take when you have a problem with getting your com-

puter to perform properly and/or getting a software application package to perform properly.

The student may list any three of these helps:

- Office Assistant
- Help Contents and Index
- What's This?
- Microsoft on the Web
- Telephone to the help line of the manufacturer of the software package; not all manufacturers have help lines, but Microsoft does have one.
- Manuals

4. Explain the relationship between ethics and software copying

    There is a direct relationship between copying software and ethics. It is unethical and even illegal to copy software except under very clear guidelines set out by the manufacturer of the software.

5. What is a computer virus? List six ways that you can protect your software from them.

    A computer virus is a computer program with unauthorized instructions that are introduced without permission or knowledge of the computer user. It is called a virus because it is contagious.

    The student may list any six of these ways to protect from a virus:

    - Educate yourself about viruses.
    - Make backups of files immediately.
    - Download only from sources you trust.
    - Install an antiviral scanning program on your system.
    - Ask the computer service professionals to alert you when a new virus occurs.
    - Do not allow programs to be loaded on your system without your authorization.
    - Purchase all software programs in tamper-proof packaging.
    - Always boot from a write-protected disk.
    - When you get a new program, write-protect the master disk before inserting it into a drive.
    - When using bulletin boards and outside programs, use a stand-alone computer.
    - Do not use unsolicited demo disks.

KEY TO CRITICAL THINKING ACTIVITY

The student is given a case and asked to answer these questions. The answers will vary; here are suggestions.

- Is there an ethical problem? If so, what is it? Yes, the supervisor has asked that the office professional make 20 copies of new software. It is unethical.
- Is there a legal problem? If so, what is it? Yes, it is also illegal to copy software.

- How should you handle the situation? Should you keep quiet and make the copies? Should you discuss the issue with your supervisor? Should you discuss the issue with you supervisor's boss? Should you talk with the team about it?

You should not keep quiet. You should tell your supervisor that it is illegal. (Maybe she doesn't know.) Tell her that you cannot copy the software. You should not do anything else unless she threatens you in some way, such as threatens your job, raise, and so forth if you do not copy it. Then you should report the situation to the Human Resources Department. If there is no solution, you should leave the company. You should not talk with the team unless you have another meeting. And, in this case, you should merely tell them that the copies are not being made since it is illegal. Since they already know the situation, there is no need to belabor the point except to make clear that you could not copy the software.

KEY TO OFFICE APPLICATIONS

OA6-1 (Goal 1)

The student is asked to team with three classmates in visiting a computer store and checking the latest applications software that is available. The findings are to be reported verbally to the class.

OA6-2 (Goal 2)

The students are to determine how to solve four software problems. Their answers will vary depending on the software they are using. They are to use the memorandum form on the student template disk to write a memo to you, giving their solutions and the resources they used to find the answers.

OA6-3 (Goals 3 and 4)

The student is to research the types of office suite software that are available and determine whether to recommend pur-

Reprinted with permission of Ergometrix, Colorado Springs, Colorado.

chasing a particular one and why. Using the memorandum form on the student template disk, the student is to write you a letter, explaining what he or she would recommend and the rationale for the recommendation. In the same memorandum the student is to explain the steps he or she would take in caring for a computer and software.

OA6-4 (Goals 3 and 4)

On page 41 of the Applications Workbook is an illustration. The student is to describe what is wrong with the picture, using what has been learned about ergonomics. Then the student is to check his or her answers on the student template disk in file OA6-4. A correct picture is provided on page 31 if you would like to enlarge it and use as an overhead.

OA6-5 (Goal 5)

The student is to prepare a flyer concerning a fitness program. The information for the flyer is in the Applications Workbook on page 42. The flyer is to be printed on half sheets of paper, with font enhancements, a border, and graphics. A copy is to be submitted to you.

Here is the text of the flyer.

JOIN OUR PHYSICAL FITNESS PROGRAM NOW!

Beginning Monday, October 15, at 4:30 p.m. in Room 335, the first session of Physical Fitness will be held. We will meet three afternoons per week for one hour—Monday, Wednesday, and Friday afternoons.

Our first session will be a get-acquainted one, with discussion centering on how future sessions will be conducted. Each session, after the initial one, will include 40 minutes of aerobic exercise and 20 minutes of information concerning proper diet and relaxation techniques.

The sessions are free. Recognition will be given to those individuals who join and complete the program.

Bring a co-worker with you and join us on Monday.

OA6-6 (Goal 5)

In the Applications Workbook on page 43 is a handwritten memo that the student is to key, making all corrections noted. The memorandum form provided on the student template disk is to be used. A copy of the memorandum is to be submitted to you. Here is the text of the memo.

TO: All Employees
FROM: Cary Alcevedos, Director
DATE: (current)
SUBJ: COMPUTER VIRUS PROTECTION

We have been notified that some computer viruses have been reported in the area recently. Many computer users transfer files to and from their office and home equipment. For this reason, it is essential that you provide protection for all of your computer sites.

Personal computers were infected last month with two viruses. The "Stoned-B1New Zealand #2" virus and the Michelangelo virus attacked the boot sector of a personal computer, making the computer inoperable. Transferring files from one computer to another allowed the viruses to spread. Viruses of this kind have the potential to destroy data on a hard disk drive.

In response to this situation, we have upgraded our virus protection software to detect and destroy these and over 2,000 other viruses. You should use the detection software immediately on all diskettes in both office and home computers to ensure they are virus free.

Contact the IS Department to obtain the detection software. Please call me at 1-3352 if you have any questions or need assistance in using the virus protection software.

KEY TO ONLINE RESEARCH APPLICATION

ORA6-7 (Goal 1)

The student is to choose two classmates to work with on this project. They are to research on the Internet the current operating systems and privacy software available. The students are to present their findings to the class.

CHAPTER 7

REPROGRAPHIC RESOURCES

Even though technology makes it possible today to have a paperless office, we have seen an increase rather than a decrease in the number of copies being made. It is important that the office worker understand how to use copiers efficiently, to select and maintain them, and to understand the ethical and legal considerations when copying materials. This chapter introduces the student to these concepts and provides experiences to help them develop expertise with reprographics. There are five goals for the student to accomplish.

STUDENT GOALS

1. Identify the types of copiers and fax machines available.
2. Explain the features available on copiers and fax machines.
3. Demonstrate knowledge of copier maintenance and selection.
4. Demonstrate an understanding of ethical and legal considerations when copying materials.
5. Use copiers.

CHAPTER OUTLINE

TEACHING SUGGESTIONS

- If you have a Kinko's or some other company that does volume copying/printing, invite a manager from the company to your class to discuss the following:
  —Types of printers that are used and special features of the printers
  —Special services such as graphics, binding, faxing, and so forth that are offered
  —Ethical and legal considerations when copying (You might ask them to share their company policy with the students.)
- If you have Xerox or some other copier manufacturer in your city, invite an executive from the company to discuss future directions of copiers; e.g., what portion of the market will multifunction units make up in the future, what are the projections for digital copiers, and so forth.
- Invite a librarian from your school to discuss what can and cannot be copied in the library. If CD's or software packages are available for checkout in the school, ask the librarian to discuss the legality of copying these items.

KEY TO SUPPLEMENTAL EXERCISE

The student is given a case on p. 49 of the Applications Workbook and asked to prepare a written report to be submitted. The student is to consider the following in the report.

- Provide an analysis of the factors that may be leading to increased copying costs.
- Give several recommendations regarding copying that may be implemented to achieve the 5-percent reduction in operating costs.

Although the answers will vary, here are suggested responses.

The factors that may be leading to increased copying costs are:

- Too many decentralized copy centers
- Lack of copy control devices on decentralized copiers
- No analysis of how decentralized copiers are being used
- Service contracts that are not cost-effective
- Possibility of too many copies being run
- Possibility of personal copies being made

Give several recommendations regarding copying that may be implemented to achieve the 5-percent reduction in operating costs.

- Before decentralized copy centers are set up, an analysis of the following factors must be made and the center must be approved by the appropriate manager:
  —The need for the center
  —How many copies will be run
  —The projected cost of the copier, supplies, and service costs

- Copy control devices could be placed on all copiers, with the manager reviewing copying costs monthly.
- Copying costs for the entire hospital could be reviewed every six months by the business manager, with questionable costs reviewed by the administrator in charge of the particular unit.

KEY TO OFFICE PROCEDURES REINFORCEMENT

1. Define the term "reprographics" and describe the four categories of copiers.

   Reprographics is the process of making copies of documents. It refers to any piece of equipment that produces multiple copies of an original document. Four categories of copiers are:

   - Low-volume copiers—These copiers typically produce from 12 to 30 copies per minute and run from 500 to 20,000 copies per month.
   - Mid-volume copiers—These copiers generate between 25 and 56 copies per minute and produce as many as 70,000 copies per month.
   - High-volume copiers—These copiers are capable of producing over 90 copies per minute, with monthly volumes from 20,000 to 150,000 copies.
   - Copier/duplicators—These machines can produce approximately 150 copies per minute, with monthly volumes of over 50,000 copies.

2. Name and describe four special features available on a copier.

   The student may name and describe any four of these special features:

   - Duplexing
   - Color reproduction
   - Document or digital editing
   - Diagnostics
   - Collate and staple
   - Interrupt key
   - Help button
   - Job recovery
   - Automatic folding
   - Touch control screen
   - Programmable memory
   - Book copy
   - Online binding
   - Image shift
   - Transparency production
   - Toner and paper changes
   - Environmentally friendly features

3. Explain how the office professional can help reduce copying abuses.

   - Do not make extra copies when they are not needed.
   - Be aware of the types of material that cannot be copied, and do not violate the law.

- Do not copy documents for your personal use.
- Do not copy cartoons, jokes, and other similar types of information to be distributed to office colleagues.
- Do not make copies of documents that you need for an outside professional group unless you have approval from your company to do so.

4. Describe the advantages and disadvantages of a centralized copy center.

Advantages

- Tighter cost controls over equipment and supplies
- Reduction of outside printing costs
- Job times at less per given task
- Less unauthorized copying

Disadvantages

- Dependence on one unit; no backups
- Higher personnel costs; dedicated operator; more walking time
- Longer total job turnaround time
- Underutilization of the equipment with some jobs

5. Explain the importance of a shredder and its relation to office technology.

With technology, copies can be made easily, and often more copies are made than are actually needed. These copies, often with confidential or sensitive information, are tossed into trashcans. People with unethical agendas can use this information to the detriment of the company. The use of a shredder can prevent the possibilities of confidential or sensitive materials getting into the hands of unauthorized persons.

KEY TO CRITICAL THINKING ACTIVITY

The student is asked to respond to these questions concerning a case. The answers will vary; here are suggested responses.

- Is what Roberto doing illegal? Yes, it is. The newsletter company specifically prohibits the copying of the material by the statement that is printed on its newsletter.
- What responsibility does the supervisor have? The supervisor is ultimately responsible since he or she is directing Roberto to make the copies.
- What should Roberto do? First, he should call the statement on the newsletter to the attention of the supervisor. Maybe the supervisor does not know that it is illegal to copy the newsletter. If the supervisor continues to insist that Roberto copy the material, he should refuse to do so, stating that since it is illegal, he cannot copy the materials. If the supervisor threatens him with firing or some other punishment, Roberto should go to the Human Resources Office to discuss the matter with the executive there. Most companies have a process for filing grievances when the supervisor is clearly overstepping his authority with the employee.

KEY TO OFFICE APPLICATIONS

OA7-1 (Goals 1 and 2)

The student is to work with four classmates, visit a technologically up-to-date office, and learn about the types of copiers and fax machines used. These questions are to be asked.

- What type of copiers do you have?
- What are the features of the copiers that you use?
- Do you use digital copiers?
- Do you use multifunction units?
- Do you have both centralized and decentralized copy centers?
- What type of fax machines do you use?
- What are the features on your fax machines?

The team is to write up their findings and submit them to you, giving the name of the organization visited. The interoffice memorandum on the student template disk is to be used in writing you a memo with the answers to the questions listed above. If there is a fax machine available to the team, they are to fax the memorandum to you. The team is to be prepared to present the findings to the class, as an oral report, if you determine that is appropriate. The team is also to write a thank-you note to the organization visited.

OA7-2 (Goal 3)

The student and two classmates are given a situation in which they are to serve on a committee to recommend a copier for the department. The team is asked to answer the following questions in a report that is to be submitted to you. Answers will vary; here are suggested responses.

- What selection criteria should be used?
  —Determine what type of materials will be copied and what sizes of paper will be needed.
  —Determine how many copies will be run per month and the projected volume over a five-year period.
  —Determine if there are space limitations for placing the copier, and if so, what they are.
  —Determine what features are needed on the copier.
  —Determine if color is needed.
  —Ask for a demonstration of several copiers.
  —Determine price, cost of supplies, and maintenance contract cost.
  —Determine the reliability of the vendor.
- Maintenance recommendations
  —Designate a key operator who will be responsible for simple repairs.
  —Train the key operator and ask to train personnel on the new copier.
  —Install a copy control device.
  —Determine whether or not a maintenance contract is cost-efficient.
  —Determine whether or not remote diagnostic systems are available.

OA7-3 (Goal 4)

The student is given a case and asked to respond to several questions. The response is to be in the form of a memorandum written to you on the form provided on the template disk. The questions, with suggested responses, are given below.

- Have you behaved ethically? Why or why not?

    No, you have not behaved ethically. You have copied material illegally, and you have been aware that you are doing so.

- Has your supervisor behaved ethically? Why or why not?

    Your supervisor has not behaved ethically if he or she has been aware that it is illegal to copy the materials. Since you have not called the illegality to the attention of your supervisor, you do not know whether or not he or she is aware. Thus, you cannot say with certainty that the supervisor has behaved unethically.

- Has the president of the company behaved ethically? Why or why not?

    Again, you do not know whether or not he or she is aware that the copying is illegal. Therefore, you cannot answer the question. Certainly, individuals in supervisory positions should be aware of the illegality; and if a lawsuit is filed by an organization, ignorance of the law is generally not a legal defense.

- What should you do about your growing concerns?

    You should talk with your supervisor immediately. If he or she tells you that it is your responsibility to do what you are told, you should then discuss the incident with the Human Resources Department. If your grievance is not considered and you continually are asked to copy materials that are illegal to copy, you should look for other employment. You do not want to work for an organization whose ethics do not match your own.

OA7-4 (Goal 5)

The student is to design the cover of an office procedures manual, using the name of the document (Office Procedures Manual) and the company name (People First International). Different type styles and graphics are to be used. Copies of the cover are to be made for the class and a copy submitted to you.

OA7-5 (Goal 5)

The student is given a section of an office procedures manual, with part of the material appearing on the template disk, file OA07-5, and revisions and additions in the Applications Workbook, pages 45–47. The document is to be revised and a copy submitted to you. Here is the revised document.

PRINTING SERVICES

<u>Overview</u>

The company provides various methods for the production of printed materials. Some regional and district offices have small, low-volume copiers; the corporate office has a centrally located mid-volume copier. The most cost-effective means of photocopying printed material exists in the company's central print shop. Not only is the cost of reproducing material cheaper in a high-volume environment, but the savings in personal time spent is perhaps even more valuable.

<u>Procedures</u>

Employees wishing to have documents/projects printed must complete a Printing Requisition (Form 33). The project will be evaluated with the specifications given, and a determination will be made by the printing technician if the job should be completed by the company's print shop or by an outside vendor. Whenever possible, the printing will be handled in-house, since this method is the most cost-effective.

<u>Services and Fees</u>

The central print shop has limitations, however, based on equipment. Criteria for selecting the method of printing are paper size, paper weight, quantity, ink color, and special finishing requirements. Generally, the budget, or cost, of a project is a major consideration. In order to assist your planning for printing requests, a list of services and fees for the central print shop is provided in this section.

The standard turnaround time needed for a simple reproduction job to be completed in the central print shop is two (2) days upon receipt of the job. However, if special paper needs to be ordered or if binding, three-hole punching, or any other finishing techniques are required, time will be added as needed. The person originating the order will always be notified of the time extension needed to complete the job. If a request is received for a job that will be printed by an outside vendor, the average time required is seven to ten (7–10) working days. More complex jobs, however, will require a longer turnaround time.

Understandably, the printing method ultimately dictates the length of time required for completion of a project. As you initiate printing requests, please take into account these considerations.

PRINT SHOP SERVICES AND FEES

Service	Fee
Collating	N/C
Collating folded sheets (per 100 sheets)	$1.00
Folding (per fold for 100 sheets)	.30
Minimum charge	3.00
Stapling (upper left or side saddle per staple)	.01
Drilling (per hole for 100 sheets)	.02
Minimum charge	2.00
Trim (per 10 cuts)	.10
Padding (per pad up to $8\frac{1}{2}''$ by $11''$)	.08
Minimum charge	1.00
Color slip sheets (per 100 sheets)	
$8\frac{1}{2}'' \times 11''$	.95
$8\frac{1}{2}'' \times 14''$	1.22
$11'' \times 17''$	1.90

KEY TO ONLINE RESEARCH APPLICATION

ORA7-6 (Goals 1 and 2)

Using the Internet, the student is to search for the latest information on copiers and fax machines. A report is to be written on the student's findings, including the sources. Students should submit their reports to you.

CHAPTER 8

THE VIRTUAL OFFICE

With millions of people working in virtual environments today, it is important that the student be introduced to the concept. As more and more businesses provide this opportunity for employees, the student may be faced with a decision as to whether or not he or she wants to work in a virtual situation. Also, as the number of people who work as independent contractors continues to increase, the student needs to be introduced to this form of work life. This chapter is designed to give the student some understanding of the virtual office.

STUDENT GOALS

1. Describe the virtual office.
2. Identify the qualities needed to be successful in a virtual environment.
3. Explain how to establish a virtual office.

CHAPTER OUTLINE

TEACHING SUGGESTIONS

- Arrange for a panel discussion among a business executive who has a number of employees telecommuting, an employee of the company who is telecommuting, and an employee who is not telecommuting but must maintain contact with the employee who is. Ask the business executive to discuss the pros and cons of telecommuting from the organizational perspective and the two employees to explain it from their individual perspectives. Ask the students to formulate questions to ask the panel during the question-and-answer period.
- Ask a sociologist in your college or university to discuss with your class the changing lifestyles, values, and family patterns of our nation and what impact these changes have on work life. If the person has expertise in the international area, ask him or her to also discuss these changes internationally.

KEY TO SUPPLEMENTAL EXERCISE

On page 51 of the Applications Workbook, the student is given a Supplemental Exercise in which he or she is asked to research the number of people who are working in virtual environments in the local city and in the nation. A graph of the statistics is to be prepared, showing the number of people in each area (virtual home environments, telecommuting full and part time) in the local city compared to the same areas in the nation. The graph is to be submitted to you.

KEY TO OFFICE PROCEDURES REINFORCEMENT

1. Describe a virtual office.

   The virtual office is a concept that originated due to the technological capability to perform work at any location and at any time. The virtual office may be any one of the following situations in which an individual is:

   - Employed by an organization and works at the organization's office for a portion of a day or a week and at his or her home for the remainder of the time
   - Employed by an organization but works full-time from the home
   - Self-employed and contracts his or her services to individual organizations
   - Self-employed and produces a product or service that is sold to the public

2. List the qualities needed in order to be successful as a virtual worker.

   - Disciplined
   - Self-starter
   - Organized
   - Creative
   - Good communicator
   - Energetic
   - Self-confident

3. Explain why understanding goals is important to the virtual worker.

   Working in a virtual environment is very different from working in the traditional office situation. If you are going to consider being a virtual worker, you need to understand your own goals and your strengths. For example, are you:

   - Independent?
   - Flexible?
   - Able to set a work schedule and maintain it?
   - Able to take control?
   - A person who needs time with children, spouse, and/or parents on a flexible basis?

   In establishing your goals, determine what your greatest strengths are, when you are happiest, what you daydream about doing, what quality-of-life results you desire, and so forth.

4. List three challenges that the virtual worker faces.

   - Isolation
   - Scope of responsibility
   - Job demands versus home demands

5. Explain how you can continue to grow professionally as a virtual worker.

   - Network with other virtual workers.
   - Join professional organizations.
   - Take classes.
   - Read.

KEY TO CRITICAL THINKING ACTIVITY

The student is given a case and asked to answer several questions. Although the answers will vary, here are suggested responses.

What suggestions do you have for Maria?

- Identify childcare sources that are available in emergency situations.
- Identify someone who can assist with the housework on a temporary basis.
- Divide the chores. Maria and her husband should each have a list of household duties that will be performed each week.
- Attend each monthly meeting unless there is a dire emergency.
- Make arrangements to have a conference call with her coworkers once each week or on an as-needed basis.
- Identify a person(s) within the organization who can help her when she needs it.
- Make arrangements to talk with her supervisor on a weekly basis.
- Move the office to a quiet area. Be certain that her family knows when she is working and when she can address family issues. Close the office door and put up a sign when working.

Should she ask to go back to the traditional office setting?

No, one month is not long enough to determine if it can work. However, Maria should give extensive thought to what her goals are, what her strengths are, and what her family needs are. It would be helpful for her to write a mission statement, detailing what she wants from life.

Should she discuss her concerns with her employer?

Yes, she should discuss her concerns but not in a self-pitying manner. She should state clearly what she needs and make suggestions for how they can be met. For example, she should ask to discuss directions and issues with her employer once a week. She should ask for a fax machine so that she can communicate better. She should tell her employer that she has identified certain people that she will be talking with concerning issues that arise and determine if her approach is satisfactory.

KEY TO OFFICE APPLICATIONS

OA8-1 (Goals 1, 2, and 3)

The student is to select two classmates to work with on this project. They are to interview two people who are working in virtual environments. These people may be discovered through the Internet, and the interview may take place online. The individuals are to respond to the following items:

- Describe your virtual office situation.
- What personal qualities are necessary in order to be successful?

- If you are a telecommuter, what does your employer provide you?
- Where is your virtual office located? What equipment do you have?
- What software do you use?
- How do you continue to grow professionally?
- What tips would you give a virtual worker?

The students are to write their findings as a team and present them orally to the class. They are to submit a written report to you.

OA8-2 (Goal 3)

The student is to write a short report (two or three pages) on how to establish a virtual office—equipment to use, software, furniture, supplies, and so forth. The student is to use periodicals as resources. The ones mentioned in this chapter may be used—*Home Office Computing, PC World,* and *PC Computing.* Resources are to be identified and the report submitted to you.

KEY TO ONLINE RESEARCH APPLICATION

ORA8-3 (Goal 3)

The student is to choose two classmates to work with on the project. Using the Internet resources given in this chapter or others that the students find, they are to determine the helps that are available online to a virtual worker. The students are to present an oral report of their findings to the class.

KEY TO END OF PART 2 ACTIVITIES

Vocabulary Review: Part 2 (Chapters 5–8)

1. OCR
2. GUI
3. microprocessor
4. CPU
5. LANs
6. mouse
7. mainframe
8. arithmetic/logic unit
9. database program
10. troubleshooting
11. operating systems software and applications software
12. bundled software programs
13. spreadsheet
14. isometric
15. virus
16. reprographics
17. decentralized copy center

18. shredder
19. fax machine
20. self-starter
21. microcomputer
22. liquid crystal display (LCD)
23. DOS
24. mission statement
25. Medicaid

Language Skills Practice: Part 2 (Chapters 5–8)

1. The memorandum was dated April 8; however, it did not reach the address until the 12th of May.
2. Eighty people will attend the seminar.
3. The address of the company is 49 North Hopkins Street.
4. It will cost $2,000 to paint the office.
5. Randall left the office some time ago.
6. The office is a mile farther down the highway.
7. Sometime today I will complete the project.
8. Engineers will soon advise the company which design should be used.
9. Please let me know when you checked all the papers.
10. It is all right for her to attend with you.
11. This reference book is yours.
12. The receptionist's desk was extremely cluttered.
13. The Edwards' women will attend the book signing.
14. The company has increased its volume of business by nearly 20 percent over the past year—no small achievement in these times.
15. He said, "The first thing to do is to acquire the habit of studying the facts"; she agreed with him.
16. The presentation that she gave was a completely new one—not the one I had heard her give previously.
17. I believe, Mary, that you will agree with me.
18. Most of his leisure time is spent at his cabin on Lake Chesdin.
19. In the excitement of the moment, I failed to tell her about the call.
20. isn't
    Rule: Do not divide contractions.
21. listen
    Rule: Avoid dividing words of six letters.
22. grounded
    Rule: The first part of a divided word must contain at least two letters; the latter part must contain at least three letters.
23. he'll
    Rule: Do not divide contractions.
24. regu-late
    Rule: Divide after a one letter syllable.
25. self-control
    Rule: Divide a hyphenated word only at the hyphen.

PART 3: OFFICE COMMUNICATION

CHAPTER 9

THE COMMUNICATION PROCESS

The chapter introduces the student to the communication process, including both verbal and nonverbal communication. Communication barriers are discussed and techniques given for reducing these barriers. The linkage between communication and self-concept is stressed. Communication growth is treated as a process, with the student cautioned that it is important to constantly evaluate and improve communication skills.

STUDENT GOALS

1. Describe the relationship between communication and self-concept.
2. Explain the communication process.
3. Identify communication barriers and techniques for reducing the barriers.
4. Use effective communication techniques.

CHAPTER OUTLINE

   I. Introduction
  II. Your Goals
 III. Communication and Self-Concept
     A. Experience
     B. Feedback from Others
        1. Vocabulary
        2. Relationships
     C. Self-Concept Strengtheners
  IV. Verbal and Nonverbal Communications
   V. The Communication Process
     A. The Originator
     B. The Message
     C. The Receiver
     D. The Response
  VI. Nonverbal Communication
     A. Body Language
     B. Voice Quality
     C. Time
     D. Space

  VII. Communication Barriers
     A. Language Usage
     B. Evaluation
     C. Allness
     D. Inference
     E. Categorization
     F. Cultural Differences
 VIII. Reduction of Communication Barriers
     A. Active Listening
     B. Person Oriented
     C. Nonjudgmental
     D. Conflict Resolution
  IX. Communication—A Growth Process
   X. Summary
  XI. Key Terms
  XII. Professional Pointers
 XIII. Office Procedures Reinforcement
 XIV. Critical Thinking Activity
  XV. Office Applications
 XVI. Online Research Application

TEACHING SUGGESTIONS

- If you have a very diverse class, invite the students to discuss their cultures. If the students are recent immigrants to the United States, ask them to discuss the differences between their native land and the United States.
- If you have an international student association in your school, invite some of the members to talk about their cultures with your class. Ask them to discuss the communication problems they have had in coming to the United States.
- Ask the students to attend a function of another culture; e.g., visit a church whose membership is primarily of a culture other than their own, a Native American activity, or a meeting of the International Club (if there is one on your campus). Ask the students to observe the communication differences and give an oral report to the class concerning these differences.

KEY TO SUPPLEMENTAL EXERCISE

The student is given a letter in the Applications Workbook on page 59 and asked to make a list of the words and phrases that affect the message in a negative or positive manner. The student is asked to rewrite the letter in a more positive tone, using the letterhead given on the student template disk. Although the responses will vary, here are suggested responses.

Negative Phrases

- your letter of complaint
- you claim that
- we cannot be responsible
- it is your responsibility
- we cannot anticipate
- we cannot train
- next time you call us, make certain that you

The letter is written in a very negative tone; there are no positive phrases—only some neutral ones.

Letter with a positive tone

Current Date

Mr. Emmett Alverez
XYZ Corporation
2358 Avenue G
Detroit, MI 48921-1879

Dear Mr. Alverez:

Your letter stating that there is a work performance issue with the recent contract employee we sent you was received in my office today. I understand that it is difficult when an employee does not perform the job to the expectations of the company. We at People First International want to assist you with finding someone who can fill your needs.

Please send me a job description of the position that you need filled. After reviewing it, I will give you a call regarding who of our pool of contractual employees will be a good fit for you. Also, I would like to talk with you about any training that we might give the prospective employee before he or she starts to work for your company.

I look forward to receiving the job description from you. I know that we will be able to provide you with an employee who will produce at the level you expect. Thank you for continuing to think of People First International when you need temporary contractual employees.

Sincerely,

KEY TO OFFICE PROCEDURES REINFORCEMENT

1. Explain the relationship between self-concept and communication.

Self-concept and communication are intrinsically linked. Self-concept is reflected in our communication, and our communication reflects our self-concept. Through communication we let other people know who we think we are. The words that we use and our body language tell others something about our self-concept.

2. Identify and explain the elements of the communication process.

   - The originator is the sender of the original message. The originator transmits information, ideas, and feelings through speaking, writing, or gesturing.
   - The message is the idea being presented by the originator. The process of turning an idea into symbols that can be communicated is called encoding. The symbols used are usually words. However, they may be gestures, such as hand signals, or a combination of words and gestures.
   - The receiver is the person for whom the message is intended. The receiver takes the symbols and decodes them into meaning.
   - The response of the receiver lets the originator know if the communication was understood.

3. List and briefly describe three types of nonverbal communication.

   The student may list any three of the following:

   - Body language. Various body motions or gestures have meaning. These meanings may not be the same in different cultures. For example, eye contact is extremely important for Americans. We tend to believe that people who do not make eye contact with us have low self-esteem, are shy, or uninterested in what we are saying. Conversely, people from Asian, Latin American, and Caribbean cultures feel that it is a sign of respect to avoid eye contact.
   - Voice quality. Tone, pitch, and pace are all nonverbal indicators present in our voice. For example, a person's voice usually will be pitched higher when he or she is tense, anxious, or nervous.
   - Time. Time has various meanings, depending on the culture. For example, being punctual is seen as important in the United States, while in Spain, Greece, Mexico, and Italy, time is not as important.
   - Space. In America, when two people are talking at close distances, we assume there is some type of close relationship. In contrast, people from Mexico and South America tend to get very close to someone when they are talking, even if that person is not a longtime friend.

4. Identify and explain three communication barriers.

   The student may identify any three of these barriers:

   - Language usage. Words taken in isolation have no meaning. They have meaning only because people have agreed upon a particular meaning. Words have different meanings in different cultures, and the meaning of words can change over time.

- Allness. Communication theorists refer to a communication problem called allness that occurs when an individual presumes that what he or she says or knows is complete, absolute, and all-inclusive.
- Inference. Inference is defined as the process of deriving logical conclusions from premises known or assumed to be true. The problem with making inferences is that individuals may act upon what they believe to be true when it is in fact not true.
- Categorization. Categorization is the ability to compare, contrast, and classify objects, persons, or ideas. Categorization can assist the learning process, but it also can block the communication process; e.g., if we assume that all people of a certain gender behave in the same way.
- Cultural differences. Since our population is becoming more diverse, we must continue to be alert to the cultural differences among us. If we are not, major communication problems can occur.

5. Explain what active listening means, and describe three suggestions for becoming an active listener.

   Active listening requires that the person listen for the meaning as well as the words of the speaker. Techniques for becoming an active listener include:

   - Preparing to listen
   - Listening for facts
   - Listening for feelings
   - Minimizing mental blocks and filters
   - Taking notes
   - Questioning and paraphrasing

KEY TO CRITICAL THINKING ACTIVITY

The student is asked to respond to these items on the situation given.

- How might Ms. Stevens help Kevin understand the image he projects?
- List the points and recommendations that Ms. Stevens should make to assist Kevin in participating in her presentations.

Here are suggested responses.

Ms. Stevens should capitalize on Kevin's strengths—his job performance, thoroughness, reliability, and competence. She should focus on his positive contribution to the office team. In order to help Kevin grow and become more self-confident, Ms. Stevens may recommend that he practice speaking more clearly and developing appropriate eye contact with the person with whom he is communicating. He should stand straight with shoulders upright. Perhaps Kevin could be asked to lead a group team project to gain practice in speaking and presenting to groups. Ms. Stevens could have Kevin explain his work or aspects of his job to someone else in the company. Communicating before groups frequently will help Kevin develop a positive self-image.

KEY TO OFFICE APPLICATIONS

OA9-1 (Goal 1)

Using the self-evaluation chart that the student completed in OA1-4, he or she is asked to choose several strengths or positive characteristics and write a one-page assessment entitled *What I Like about Myself.* The student is to share the evaluation with a trusted family member or friend.

OA9-2 (Goals 2 and 3)

Students are asked to participate in a group perception activity. The class is to divide into groups of eight, with members describing their individual perceptions of a picture provided by you. The picture can be from a current newspaper or magazine; it should show engagement or action, diversity of individuals, and group interaction, if possible. Once the exercise is completed, the groups are asked to discuss these two questions.

- How did the differences in the perceptions of various members interfere with the communication process?
- What contributes to these various perceptions?

OA9-3 (Goals 3 and 4)

The student is to complete a form on nonverbal behavior provided on pages 57 and 58 of the Applications Workbook. Answers are to be compared with one classmate, with differences and similarities of nonverbal behavior noted. You might want the students to present their findings orally to the class.

KEY TO ONLINE RESOURCE APPLICATION

ORA9-4 (Goals 3 and 4)

Students are to work with two classmates on this project. Using the Internet, they are to research communication patterns in Japan, Mexico, and Africa. Findings are to be presented orally to the class.

CHAPTER 10

WRITTEN COMMUNICATIONS

As an office professional, the student will be expected to compose correspondence. In some situations, the composition function will be limited to routine correspondence; in other situations, the office professional may compose and/or draft a majority of the correspondence that leaves the office. This chapter is designed to help the student understand and apply effective writing principles when composing letters, email, memorandums, and reports. Since collaborative writing is done in the workplace today, there is a section on collaborative writing and an office application that involves writing collaboratively.

STUDENT GOALS

1. Apply effective writing principles when composing email, memorandums, letters, and reports.
2. Compose business correspondence.
3. Write collaboratively.

CHAPTER OUTLINE

TEACHING SUGGESTIONS

- Ask each member of the class to collect two or three business letters and analyze their effectiveness in an oral report to the class.
- Have the students critique each other's work when writing letters and reports in this chapter. This type of assignment has a twofold purpose—helping them to work in teams and to learn from each other in the writing process.
- Present the students with a list of words that we use. Ask them to rate the words on a scale of 1 to 5, with 5 having a positive connotation and 1 having a negative connotation. Some possible words for you to use are given here. Once the students rate the list you give them, ask them to work in teams to prepare their own lists of positive and negative words. The purpose of this exercise is to help them understand the importance of using positive words, rather than negative ones.

    Sibling
    Brat
    Athlete
    Jock
    Aggressive
    Assertive
    Girl
    Woman
    Workplace
    Sweat Shop
    Cheap
    Inexpensive

KEY TO SUPPLEMENTAL EXERCISE

In the Applications Workbook, on pages 63–67, edited copy of a report on preparing office manuals is given. The student is to key the report in final form, making all changes. There are words in the copy that are misspelled and not noted. The student is reminded to correct all spelling errors. The student is also to prepare a title page for this report, using graphics, borders, or other types of enhancements. The corrected copy is shown here. Title pages will vary as to format; the information on the title page is to include the report title, the student's name as author of the report, and the current date.

PREPARING OFFICE MANUALS

Office manuals are formal communications of management's objectives that are developed to acquaint employees with the policies and practices of a company. They are also used to assign responsibility for performing certain duties and to establish procedures for those duties. A well-written office manual saves time for both management and the employee. It provides valuable information in printed form and eliminates the need for repetitive instructions. Office manuals should be written in a readable style, prepared economically, and distributed to each employee.

Types of Manuals

There are four types of office manuals commonly found; they are:

1. Policy Manual. This manual contains decisions, resolutions, and pronouncements of company policies established by the board of directors.
2. Organization Manual. This manual provides an explanation of the organization, duties, and responsibilities of various departments.
3. Administrative Practice Manual. Standard procedures and methods for performing the company's work are given in this manual.
4. Departmental Practice Manual. This manual contains procedures for a particular department dealing with the internal policies, organization, and work methods of that department.

The types of manuals prepared and used within a company depend on the size of the company, the number of departments in the company, the work performed in each department, and the centralization or decentralization of the company.

General Information in Office Manuals

Office manuals are not uniformly organized. There is, however, certain information pertaining to personnel policies that should be present in all office manuals. They should include some statement as to how employees are hired, the difference between part-time and full-time employment, information about performance evaluations, and salary increases, as well as other general personnel information. For the sake of simplicity, a discussion of this information is presented in alphabetical order.

Absence. This section of an office manual should state clearly company policies regarding absences of employees. It should explain whether employees are paid for absences and to whom they should report in case of absence.

Accidents. There should be an explanation of the workers' compensation law if the company is protected by such a law. Employees should be instructed to report immediately any personal accidents while working, even though the accident may seem trivial at first.

Attendance. Employees should be told the importance of regular attendance and punctuality. If the company keeps a record of attendance and punctuality to be used in evaluating employees for promotion, employees should be so informed.

Change of address. Employees should be told that the personnel department keeps a record of the name, home address, and telephone number of each employee. In case of change, the personnel department should be notified immediately.

Credit Union. If the company has a credit union for the convenience of employees, detailed information about participation should be made available.

Education. Each employee should be reminded that previous education plays a prominent part in selecting a person for a particular job. Employees are to be reminded that detailed information about their educational experiences is kept on file and used as a basis for advancement and promotion. If the company has a plan for paying part or all the tuition of employees who wish to further their education, the plan should be explained. Employees should be encouraged to discuss further educational possibilities with their immediate supervisors.

Group Insurance. If the company has an insurance plan for employees, the plan should be outlined, or the employees should be told that detailed information will be provided at a certain time.

Hospitalization. If the company has a plan where employees can take advantage of the services offered by a medical service organization, the plan should be explained.

Performance Evaluations. Employees should be told of periodic evaluations that are done by supervisors and by the personnel department.

Personal Mail. The attitude of the company toward employees receiving personal mail at the company address should be explained.

Probationary Periods. If the company assumes that employees are placed on probation for a period of three to six months after initial employment, it should be explained.

Salary. Employees should be told when and how they will be paid. Policies regarding salary increases should be explained, along with the importance of keeping salary matters confidential.

Special Needs. Employees with disabilities that require special needs should be notified of the company's obligations to meet their needs.

Telephone. An explanation of making and receiving personal telephone calls while at work should be given.

Vacations. Vacation policies should be explained for both full-time and part-time employees.

One of the greatest difficulties in preparing office manuals for employees is obtaining agreement from company executives on what practices and policies should be included. If only departmental manuals are involved, the development of the manual is usually initiated and supervised by the office in charge of that department. If more elaborate manuals are planned, one person should probably assume complete charge in planning them—outlining procedures for preparation, editing, publishing, distributing, and revising manuals. Whatever the format, office manuals should be prepared so that material can be easily inserted. A well-organized office manual can prove to be an invaluable aid for employees.

KEY TO OFFICE PROCEDURES REINFORCEMENT

1. Name and explain the common characteristics of effective correspondence.

The student should name and explain these characteristics:

- Complete
- Clear
- Accurate
- Prompt
- Concise
- Courteous
- Positive

2. Explain the planning steps of correspondence.

The planning steps are:

- Analyze the reader. By evaluating the reader correctly, one is able to communicate more effectively and to have the message understood more completely.
- Determine the purpose. What should the document accomplish? What should the reader do after reading the document? What does the reader need to know?
- Organize the content. The writer should plan the paragraphs, use appropriate sentence structure, eliminate the passive voice, determine the readability level, and utilize software-writing aids.

3. What is passive voice? Why should it be used sparingly?

Passive voice is present when the subject of the sentence receives the action or is acted upon. It should be used sparingly because it is not generally as strong or as clear as the active voice. When correspondence is written totally in the passive voice, it is much more difficult to read and understand.

4. Explain the difference between primary and secondary research.

Primary research is the original collection of data; this data may be collected through surveys, observations, and/or experiments. Secondary research is collecting information and/or data through resources such as the library or the Internet.

5. What is an executive summary?

An executive summary is a one- or two-page summary of the report. It is written for the busy executive who does not need to have a detailed understanding of all aspects of the report, but does need to know the background, major findings, and recommendations.

KEY TO CRITICAL THINKING ACTIVITY

The student is given a case and asked to answer several questions. Although the answers will vary, here are suggested responses.

- Should Darlene admit that she does not keep busy and that her workload is too light?

Yes, Darlene should tell her employer that her workload is light.

- How could Darlene approach Mr. Stevenson to discuss a better utilization of her skills?

  Darlene should suggest that she could assist in composing some of the correspondence. She should indicate that she enjoys writing and believes her skills are good.

- What specific responsibilities could Darlene assume for Mr. Stevenson?

  She can complete routine forms, such as those for patents. Darlene can respond to routine requests for information about new products if given the proper amount of information.

- How would you react to a situation such as this one? Would you want to increase your workload?

  Students' answers will differ. Look for willingness on the part of students to assume additional responsibilities.

KEY TO OFFICE APPLICATIONS

OA10-1 (Goals 1 and 2)

The student is to load the file 10-1 from the student template disk and analyze the memorandum for words or phrases that are inappropriate. The student is to highlight these words by using bold format and print a copy. The student is then to revise the memorandum and print a final copy.

Unsuitable words and phrases

You are hereby notified
an additional pay
same commitment regarding
at the company's discretion
deem
aforementioned
without hesitation or delay

MEMORANDUM

TO: Department Managers
FROM: Wanda Foster
DATE: May 1,—
SUBJECT: Implementation of New Personnel Policy

Effective Monday, June 1,—, evening shift employees will receive a pay increase. The increase will be based on a percentage of the current salary scale. Employees having served the company ten or more years will receive a 4-percent increase; five to nine years, a 3-percent increase; and less than five years, a 2-percent increase.

Health and dental benefits will remain the same for all employees. If you wish to make changes in other deductions, let the Personnel Department know by May 15.

OA10-2 (Goals 1 and 2)

The student is to use the email form on the student data template disk in file OA10-2 to write an email message to Elaine Bordeaux of the Paris, France, office, requesting copies of the Income and Expense Statement for the last two years. Elaine's email address is eb@pfi.com. Mr. Menendez needs this information within two weeks. Here is a sample email:

TO: eb@pfi.com

SUBJ: Copy of Income and Expense Statement for Last Two Years

Please send Mr. Menendez one copy of the Income and Expense Statements for the France office for the last two years by _____ (one week from current date).

Thank you.

(Student's name)

OA10-3 (Goals 1 and 2)

The student has been asked to speak at the local IAAP chapter on "Effective Written Communication Techniques." The student will not be able to do so due to the heavy office workload at the present time. The student is to write a letter declining the invitation, but suggesting that he or she will be able to do so at a later time.

OA10-4 (Goals 1, 2, and 3)

The student is to choose three classmates to work with on this project. They are to conduct primary research by surveying 15 to 20 students on one of the three issues given below. A report is to be written of their findings, using charts and graphs. If the students developed a written survey, they are to provide a copy of the survey as an appendix to their report. After they finish writing the report, they are to use the evaluation form in the Applications Workbook on pages 61 and 62 to determine if the team worked together successfully. A copy of the report is to be submitted to you, along with the team evaluation form. Students may choose one of the following issues for their survey:

- Are ethics a problem in our society?
- Is it okay to lie under oath?
- Should there be censure of material on the Internet?

KEY TO ONLINE RESEARCH APPLICATION

ORA 10-5 (Goals 1 and 2)

Using the Internet, the student is to research the characteristics of effective messages. A memo is to be written to you, using the memorandum form provided on the student template disk. A short summary of the material is to be submitted, along with a listing of the resources. The student is to use this format when listing resources: Bowers, K. L. (November 2000). *Effective Letters,* http://www.dev.com. (All of this information is not available for all Internet resources; however, the student is to document carefully, using the information available.)

CHAPTER 11

PRESENTATIONS

This chapter focuses on presenting letters and reports effectively so that the recipient will want to read the correspondence. Since the office professional is called upon occasionally to present oral presentations as part of a team or as an individual, the chapter also concentrates on developing oral communication skills.

STUDENT GOALS

1. Prepare letters and reports using appropriate style and placement.
2. Prepare and deliver oral presentations.

CHAPTER OUTLINE

I. Introduction
II. Your Goals
III. Presenting Letters
   A. Letter Parts
      1. Letter Styles and Punctuation
      2. Punctuation Styles
      3. Stationery
      4. Envelopes
      5. Mailability
IV. Presenting Reports
   A. Documentation
      1. Footnotes and Endnotes
      2. Internal Citations
      3. Internet Citations
      4. Bibliography or Reference Section
   B. Graphics
   C. Clip Art, Line Drawings, and Borders
   D. Margins and Page Numbers
   E. Headings
   F. Quotations
V. Researching and Keying Presentations
VI. Preparing and Delivering Oral Presentations
   A. Determine the Purpose
   B. Determine the Anticipated Audience
   C. Determine the Setting
   D. Gather the Material
   E. Organize the Presentation
   F. Develop an Opening

   G. Use Powerful Language
   H. Develop a Strong Closing
   I. Pay Attention to Body Language
   J. Use Visual Aids
   K. Dress Appropriately
   L. Rehearse the Presentation
   M. Control Nervousness
   N. Critique Your Presentation
VII. Presenting as a Team
VIII. Summary
IX. Key Terms
X. Professional Pointers
XI. Office Procedures Reinforcement
XII. Critical Thinking Activity
XIII. Office Applications
XIV. Online Research Application

TEACHING SUGGESTIONS

- Invite a speech teacher from your college to provide pointers to your class on delivering oral presentations.
- Ask the students to attend one or two oral presentations (in teams of three), critique the presentation, and present their critique to the class.
- Bring in several good secretarial reference books and review the contents with the class; let the class members know that it is important to have adequate reference materials available on their desk in the office.

KEY TO SUPPLEMENTAL EXERCISE

The student is given a supplemental exercise in the Applications Workbook on page 71. The student is to send a letter, on the student template disk in file SE11a, to four individuals. There are errors in the copy that must be corrected. Letterhead is provided on the student template disk.

The letter is to go to the following individuals:

- Dr. K. A. Lepzinski
Kirchhoff Consultants
906 Lake Drive
Royal Oak, MI 48068

- Mr. Arthur B. Mullennix
  Melching, Inc.
  2110 Fuller
  Southfield, MI 48075
- Ms. Alana Steeby
  The Gerritt Company
  1370 Buttrick SE
  Detroit, MI 48142
- Mr. John Vrona
  Bertsch Company
  6906 Riverview Drive
  Detroit, MI 48201

(Inside address)

Dear (appropriate name)

Trends in the global marketplace are creating opportunities for investment that are unparalleled. The International Business Association is planning an economic development conference on April 24–25. As a nationally recognized expert, your view would be very important to our audience.

Would you be willing to participate in a panel discussion on the afternoon of the 24th. The topic will be Latin-American Trade Practices and Opportunities. The panel will consist of four people. We would like for each individual presentation to be approximately 15 minutes in length, with a 30-minute question and answer session.

Please let me know by May 10 if you will be able to accept this invitation. I hope your schedule will permit your doing so. Your knowledge and vision of the area will help the conference be a success.

Sincerely,

Juan Menendez
Vice President of International Operations

pc

   Errors in the copy were: "is" for "are" in the first sentence and "unparalleled" misspelled. Fourth sentence included one error—"24" for "24th." Seventh sentence included one error: "30 minute" for "30-minute." Ninth sentence included one error: "you" for "your."

KEY TO OFFICE PROCEDURES REINFORCEMENT

1. Explain two types of letter and punctuation styles.
   - Block style letter—all lines start at the left margin
   - Modified block style letter—the date and complimentary close begin at the approximate center of the letter; paragraphs may be indented or blocked
   - Open punctuation—no punctuation after the salutation or complimentary close
   - Mixed punctuation—a colon after the salutation and a comma after the complimentary close

2. Define mailability and list eight items you should check when proofreading a letter for mailability.

   Mailability means that the letter is free of any type of error. When proofreading for mailability, you should ask these questions. (The student may list any eight of the following questions.)

   - Is the format correct?
   - Have you used an appropriate letter style and punctuation style?
   - Is the dateline appropriately placed? Is the date correct?
   - Is the salutation correct? Is it appropriately placed?
   - Are the complimentary close and signature lines correct and appropriately placed?
   - Are the reference initials in the appropriate place?
   - If there are enclosures, have they been noted on the letter?
   - If there are special letter parts such as attention lines, are they correct and appropriately placed?
   - If a copy is to be sent to another individual, is it noted on the letter in the appropriate place?
   - Does the envelope address match the letter address?
   - Is the appropriate envelope format used?
   - Is the letter free of grammatical and punctuation errors? Is it free of misspelled words? (Have you used your grammar and spell check program?)
   - Is the letter folded and inserted in the envelope correctly?

3. Explain the difference between footnotes and internal citations.

   - Footnotes are documentation of reference sources used; they appear as superscripts in the manuscript, with the information about the reference (author, title of work, publisher, date, and page number) at the bottom of the page where the superscript(s) appears.
   - Internal citations are also documentation of reference sources used. However, only the author's name and date (APA style) or author's name and page number (MLA style) appear on the page where the reference is noted. No superscript number appears. Detailed information about the work appears at the end of the manuscript under a section entitled "Works Cited," "Reference List," or "Notes."

4. List five elements that you should consider when planning graphics.

   The student may list any five of the following elements.

   - Who is the audience?
   - Will graphics assist the audience in understanding the message?
   - What purpose will the graphic(s) serve?
   - Are you presenting the information in the graphics in a straightforward manner?
   - Is the graphic placed appropriately?
   - Has the appropriate type of graphic been selected?

- Will color help get the message of the graphic across to the reader?

5. List ten steps you should take when planning and giving an oral presentation.

The student may list any ten of the following steps.

- Determine the purpose
- Determine the anticipated audience
- Determine the setting
- Gather the material
- Organize the presentation
- Develop an opening
- Use powerful language
- Develop a strong closing
- Pay attention to body language
- Use visual aids
- Dress appropriately
- Rehearse the presentation
- Control nervousness
- Critique your presentation

KEY TO CRITICAL THINKING ACTIVITY

The student is given a case and asked to answer these questions. Although the answers will vary, here are suggested responses.

- What suggestions would you make to Glenna for improvement?
  — Continue to use spell check, but also proofread carefully for errors that the spell check doesn't catch. Ask someone to cover the phones, and choose a quiet place to proofread where there are fewer interruptions. Glenna may also ask another office professional to help her proofread the letters.
  — Purchase a reference book that shows examples of letters for various situations.
  — Ask Mr. Tyler to give her a list of the valuations, with the taxpayers' names; check the figures in the valuations against the figures Mr. Tyler gives her and the spelling of the taxpayers' names.
  — Ask someone in the office who writes well to help her write a negative message in a positive tone. If there is no one in the office who can help, take a short course in letter composition.
- How might office efficiency and effectiveness be improved?
  — Mr. Tyler might consider delegating some of the letter reading and even signing to another executive within the office. It probably is not important for him to sign each letter. If it is important that Mr. Tyler sign each letter, he can ask an executive to proofread the letters before he signs them.
  — During the period in which Glenna is working on valuation letters, she may ask for assistance with her other duties so that she can give quality time to proofing the letters well.

KEY TO OFFICE APPLICATIONS

OA11-1 (Goal 1)

The student is to key the handwritten letter that appears in the Applications Workbook on pages 69 and 70. The student is to use the letterhead appearing on the student template disk. Errors are in the letter and the format is not appropriate. The student is to make the necessary changes.

Current Date

Mr. Bruce Cloninger
Placement Representative
Computer Institute
901 West Franklin Street
Detroit, MI (No ZIP code is given in the rough draft; the student is to put in the ZIP code by getting a ZIP code directory and selecting one of the Detroit ZIP codes from the directory.)

Dear Mr. Cloninger:

People First International has a need for individuals who are interested in a computer career. The Computer Development Program is an intensive two-year training program that provides the industry knowledge and technical expertise needed for success in our environment. Candidates must have a degree in business, with specialization in computers, an above-average grade point average, a track record of leadership ability, and a willingness to relocate within the United States or to international sites in France and Germany.

The long-term growth picture for People First International is excellent. We expect to employ fifty new employees this year. We anticipate maintaining this level of staffing in the future.

Enclosed for your information are the following materials:

- Computer Development Program Description
- People First International Employee Guide
- Benefit Summary
- A brochure entitled *Success in Business with People First, International*

I welcome the opportunity to talk further with interested students. If you have any questions regarding People First International, please contact me at 313 555 0199.

Sincerely,

Kyle Kronan
Corporate Recruiter

KK/ms/clon/11.20

Enclosures (4)

OA11-2 (Goal 1)

The student is to select three classmates to work with on this office application. They are to research and prepare a report on one of the following topics:

- Student Use of the Internet
- Sexual Harassment in the Workplace
- Communication Patterns of Different Nationalities

The students may also select another topic (not on the list) if approved by you. They are to conduct primary and secondary research on the topic and prepare a report that has the following parts:

- Title Page
- Executive Summary
- Body
- Footnotes, endnotes, or internal citations
- Reference section
- Appendices

The students are to do a draft copy of the report before keying the final version; the report is to be bound.

OA11-3 (Goals 1 and 2)

As a team (with the same classmates who worked together in OA11-2), the report prepared in OA11-2 is to be presented to the class. Students are to use:

- Presentation software (if available) or some type of visuals
- The techniques presented in this chapter on delivering effective oral presentations

An evaluation sheet is to be prepared and submitted to the class to evaluate the presentation. This evaluation is not to be submitted to you unless you ask for it; it is for the students' growth. The student is to submit the written report to you.

KEY TO ONLINE RESEARCH APPLICATION

ORA11-4 (Goal 1)

The student is asked to prepare a report on the state of Michigan for 15 employees who will be transferred to People First International from the Atlanta office. The report is to include the following topics, along with any others that the student thinks are important to include.

- Geographic size
- Population
- Climate
- Economic development (major employers of types of business and industry)
- Legislative representatives (U.S. Senate and House of Representatives)
- School system
- Cultural activities

The student is to use the Internet in researching the topic. A report is to be prepared of the findings and submitted to you.

CHAPTER 12

TELECOMMUNICATION SKILLS

As an office professional, the student will be expected to have an understanding of telecommunications and how it affects businesses. This chapter is designed to expose students to general information regarding networks, telecommunications equipment and systems and electronic messages. It also describes factors to consider when selecting telephone systems. Office professionals have a variety of responsibilities with regard to the telephone. The chapter details appropriate telephone techniques, specific tactics for dealing with incoming telephone calls as well as guidelines for placing outgoing calls. Types of long-distance services are described with guidelines for choosing the appropriate ones.

STUDENT GOALS

1. Explain how telecommunications affects the way information is transmitted through networks.
2. Identify telecommunications equipment and services.
3. Develop and use proper telephone techniques.
4. Discuss the impact of telecommunications in the office.

CHAPTER OUTLINE

I. Introduction
II. Your Goals
III. Communications Yesterday and Today
IV. Networks
    A. Types of Networks
    B. Local Area Networks (LANs)
    C. Wide Area Networks (WANs)
    D. Wireless Networks
V. Network Connections
    A. Modems
    B. Integrated Services Digital Network (ISDN)
    C. Digital Subscriber Line (DSL)
    D. Cable Modems
VI. Telecommunications Equipment and Systems
    A. The Telephone
    B. Switching Systems
        1. Key Systems
        2. PBX Systems
        3. Centrex

    C. Telephone Equipment
        1. Single-Line Telephones
        2. Multiline Telephones
        3. Optional Telephone Features
        4. Optional Telephone Services
    D. Special Telephone Equipment
        1. Cellular Telephones
        2. Portable Pagers
        3. Cordless Telephones
    E. Electronic Messages
    F. Unified Messaging
    G. Videophones
    H. Selection of a Telephone System
VI. Telephone Responsibilities
    A. Telephone Techniques
        1. Develop a Pleasant Voice
        2. Speak Distinctly
        3. Be Helpful and Discreet
        4. Ask Questions Tactfully
        5. Take Messages Completely and Accurately
        6. Be Attentive
        7. Avoid Slang
        8. Use the Caller's Name
        9. Transfer Calls Properly
        10. Terminate Calls Courteously
        11. Keep a List of Frequently Called Numbers
        12. Handle Problem Calls
    B. Incoming Calls
        1. Answer Promptly
        2. Identify Yourself and/or the Company
        3. Be Prepared
        4. Place Calls on Hold Only After Requesting Permission
        5. Handle Multiple Calls
        6. Screen Calls
        7. Leave a Message When You Leave Your Desk
        8. Follow Through on Promises
        9. Keep a Log of Incoming Calls
    C. Outgoing Calls
        1. Plan Your Call
        2. Know the Number
        3. Allow Time to Answer
        4. Keep a Record of Outgoing Calls

TEACHING SUGGESTIONS

- Ask each member of the class to discuss the types of telecommunication equipment he or she owns (or has experience using) and describe his or her experiences to the class.
- Ask someone from within your organization to discuss the telephone system and its setup.
- Break the students into pairs and practice using the techniques for handling incoming calls and placing outgoing calls in an office. It may be helpful to provide the students with specific situations to use.
- Break the students into groups and have each group develop a "problem" telephone call and two ways of handling it. After all groups have developed their situation, have them switch scenarios and write a response as to how to deal with the caller.

KEY TO SUPPLEMENTAL EXERCISE

An additional exercise is provided in the Applications Workbook. The students are to write a brief script of how they would respond to four telephone calls. Although responses will vary, here are some suggestions.

1. "Ms. Albright, do I remember correctly that you are with Heminway Corporation? It's good to hear from you again. Mr. Alexander is unable to take calls; may I give him a message or refer your call to someone who is available?"
2. "If you will tell me your name and the nature of your call, I will immediately find someone who can assist you."
3. The customer is upset, so let him talk without interruption. Usually an angry person will calm down after the initial explosion if the listener reacts calmly. An appropriate response would be, "Mr. Shields, I understand your concern. May I take your number and have Mr. Alexander call you as soon as he returns, or can someone else help you?"

4. "I'm sorry you are delayed in traffic, Ms. Arlston. Mr. Alexander is on a long-distance call, so I cannot put you through to him. I know that he has a commitment at 3 p.m. today. Is there another time that you could meet with him?"

KEY TO OFFICE PROCEDURES REINFORCEMENT

1. Describe the differences between the three main types of networks.

   A local area network links various types of equipment used within a building or several buildings within the same geographic area. It consists of transmission cable to transmit the information, plus interface units to link the various pieces of equipment to the cable.

   Wide area network connections may be established through the public telephone network. The WAN connections link independent local area networks that may be from city to city, across the nation, or global. A combination of telephone lines and satellites transmit the information.

   Wireless networks work off satellites without connections to traditional telephone lines. This technology allows network communication anywhere in the world without traditional wiring or a telephone jack.

2. Name and describe three optional telephone services.

   Optional telephone services include the following:

   - Call waiting
   - Caller ID
   - Call forwarding
   - Conferencing calling
   - Dialing features
   - Voice messaging

3. Describe the advantages of voice messaging over a standard telephone answering machine.

   Advantages of voice mail include the following:

   - Increases speed of communications by getting messages through even when there are time zone differences.
   - Increases productivity by eliminating repeated telephone calls
   - Decreases extraneous conversation
   - Provides opportunities to communicate with the office at any time
   - Decreases internal memorandums to individuals or groups

4. Explain unified messaging and its impact on future electronic communications.

   Unified messaging integrates voice, email, and fax messaging. One mailbox will include the message in all three formats. The user can then choose any of the formats to retrieve and respond to messages.

5. Explain how to place outgoing calls efficiently.

   Know the telephone number of the person being called by keeping an up-to-date file or checking with directory assistance as needed. Allow the phone to ring six to eight times in order to give the person adequate time to answer. Know the purpose of your call in advance. Keep a record of outgoing calls. Use long-distance services properly, and remember the differences in time zones.

KEY TO CRITICAL THINKING ACTIVITY

1. To begin her study of a voice-mail system for the law firm, Latonya should first survey all employees. She should determine what problems, if any, others experience with the current telephone system. It would be helpful to know the average number of calls each person receives and the number of messages that are taken. The nature of most messages might be beneficial to record; for example, do many callers just want to leave information without having to speak to the attorneys, or do the attorneys have to return the majority of the phone calls themselves? Latonya should record as many facts from as many employees as possible about the current situation.

2. After summarizing the needs of the office, Latonya should call several companies that sell voice-mail systems. Most companies are very eager to send a representative to explain various systems and their capabilities. It would also be helpful to question other law firms or companies that have voice mail to learn the advantages and disadvantages of their systems.

3. Latonya should select the features of a system that would benefit the law firm the most. For example, messages can be left 24 hours a day; a client can leave a message directly in the attorney's voice mailbox, rather than leaving repeated messages with the receptionist. Because messages get through, the length of calls is shortened; and voice mail helps to reduce the number of internal memorandums.

KEY TO OFFICE APPLICATIONS

OA12-1 (Goals 1 and 4)

Student are to write a short report (two or three pages) summarizing three articles on one of the three networking topics that are listed. These are:

Local Area Networks
Wide Area Networks
Wireless Networks

In addition, students should submit a memorandum to you indicating why they chose the topic and how they might use the information they obtained in their present job or a future job.

OA12-2 (Goal 2)

The student is to work with two classmates on this project. The students are to contact two cellular telephone service providers in their area and ask them the following questions.

- Is it possible to purchase analog service, digital service, or both?
- What kinds of enhanced features are available with the cellular telephone?
- How far can you travel before you are charged roaming fees?
- What are the rates for peak and off-peak calls?
- Are there any other fees associated with the telephone?
- Are there any "perks" or special deals that come with the telephone?
- What kind of contract must be signed?
- What is the penalty for breaking a contract?

Students are to present their findings orally to the class. In addition, the students should prepare a written report for you that summarizes their findings as well as indicates which cellular phone service provider they would choose along with supporting information for that decision.

OA12-3 (Goal 3)

Students are to supply information that is missing on telephone messages. Appropriate answers to the questions are as follows:

1. The area code for Shreveport, Louisiana, is 318.
2. North Platte is located in Nebraska.
3. Princeton University is located in Princeton, New Jersey. The area code is 609.
4. If the home office in Detroit, MI, must fax a document to the Atlanta office by noon their time, the fax must be sent by 12 noon. (There are no differences in time zones. Both offices are on Eastern time.)
5. There is no international directory assistance number. The long-distance operator assists in obtaining international numbers.

OA12-4 (Goal 3)

The students are to analyze the telephone call and answer the following questions. Student answers will vary but should include the following kinds of information.

1. Was the telephone call effective? Why or why not?

   The telephone call was not effective for several reasons. (1) Gloria was not very courteous with the caller: she put him on hold without first asking permission, she did not use his name, and she seemed abrupt and uncaring. (2) Gloria made the caller give all of the information without asking the appropriate questions. (3) She claimed not to have responsibility for shipping, and she instructed the caller to call that department himself. (4) She warned the caller to pay the bill anyway in order to avoid a finance charge. (5) She told him to call her supervisor tomorrow instead of offering to have the supervisor call *him* back at a certain time.

2. What could Gloria have done differently in the beginning of the conversation that would have set a better tone for the conversation?

   To begin with, she should have asked him if he could hold while she answered the other line. She should not have kept him on hold for so long, and she should have apologized for having done so. She could have asked more questions and seemed concerned about the caller's problem instead of acting like she didn't care. She should have offered to contact the appropriate departments or to transfer the caller to those departments. If this didn't satisfy the caller, she should have offered to have her supervisor call him, and she should have asked the caller to let her know of a good time when he could be reached.

3. According to information presented in the chapter, list all the mistakes that Gloria made in handling this telephone call.

   She didn't get the conversation off to a positive start. Instead, she put the caller on hold without asking his permission first. She then kept him on hold for five minutes instead of coming back to let him know that she would be on the other call for a while longer. She did not use his name at all in the conversation. She did not ask questions tactfully. In fact, it was up to the caller to explain most of the problem. She did not seem to be courteous and considerate. She told the caller it was his responsibility to contact the shipping department as well as her supervisor. In addition, she advised him to pay the bill—for merchandise he had never received. In general, this was a problem call, and Gloria did not handle if effectively.

4. Rewrite the conversation in a way that corrects all mistakes you identified in question 3.

   Student answers to this section will vary. Students should incorporate their answers from questions 1–3 in this answer. All mistakes listed in question 3 should be corrected in the rewritten conversation.

Gloria:	XYZ Office Supplies, this is Gloria. May I place you on hold for a moment. I must answer another phone; I will be back shortly.
Gloria:	Thank you for waiting. How can I help you?
Mr. Silva:	This is Hector Silva and you can help me by taking care of my problem.
Gloria:	I'll be happy to help you, if I can.
Mr. Silva:	Well, I ordered two dozen printer ribbons three weeks ago and they still are not here. Better yet, I got the bill for them today and it says that it is already past due.
Gloria:	Let me check on this for you, Mr. Silva. Can you give me the order number from the bill?
Mr. Silva:	The order number is 15432.
Gloria:	You can ignore the bill until the ribbons arrive. I'll talk to accounting and make sure the finance charge is removed. I'll need to check with shipping and see when they were scheduled to be shipped. This make take a few minutes, would you like to hold or can I call you back?
Mr. Silva:	Thank you very much. You can call me. My number is 783-555-1432.

OA12-5 (Goals 3 and 4)

Students are to design a form to be used in evaluating telephone service. A sample form appears below.

TELEPHONE SERVICE EVALUATION FORM

Date of Call: Time of Call:

Branch Office Called: Department Called:

Was the call answered promptly (within 3 rings)?	Yes _____	No _____
Was the call placed on hold?	Yes _____	No _____
If yes, was permission asked before placing the call on hold?	Yes _____	No _____
Was the call transferred to another extension?	Yes _____	No _____
If yes, was the transfer handled properly?	Yes _____	No _____
If no, please explain.		

Was the caller's name used during the transaction?	Yes _____	No _____
Were questions answered completely and courteously?	Yes _____	No _____
If no, please explain.		

_____

How many employees did the caller have to speak with before completing the purpose of the call?
   Please circle   1   2   3   4   other_____

Overall Rating: Excellent _____   Very Good _____   Good _____   Poor _____

Comments:

KEY TO ONLINE RESEARCH APPLICATION

ORA12-6

Using the Internet, students are to research two long-distance service providers. They are to compare their business telephone rates and packages and find out what kinds of networking opportunities and equipment they provide. Students should submit this information to you in the form of a report.

CHAPTER 13

OFFICE MAIL

The amount of mail received by companies today is on the increase rather than the decrease. In fact, statistics show that mail volume has increased over 300 percent in the past two decades. The cost of handling this increased mail has become a significant expense to business. This chapter is designed to assist the office professional in understanding how to handle both incoming and outgoing mail.

STUDENT GOALS

1. Identify mail classifications and mail services.
2. Process outgoing mail.
3. Process incoming mail.
4. Describe projected future mail trends.

CHAPTER OUTLINE

   I. Introduction
  II. Your Goals
 III. U.S. Postal Mail Services
     A. Postal Service Classifications
       1. Express Mail
       2. Priority Mail
       3. First-Class Mail
       4. Periodicals
       5. Standard Mail (A)
       6. Standard Mail (B)
       7. Parcel Post
     B. Special Mail Services
       1. Certificate of Mailing
       2. Registered Mail
       3. Restricted Delivery
       4. Return Receipt
       5. Collect on Delivery (COD)
       6. Certified Mail
       7. Insured Mail
       8. Money Order
       9. Authorization to Hold Mail
     C. International Mail
  IV. Private Mail Services
   V. Electronic Messages
     A. Email
     B. Fax Mail
     C. Telegrams

  VI. Outgoing Mail
     A. Check Enclosures
     B. Prepare Envelopes
       1. Address Envelopes
       2. Adhere to Automation Requirements
     C. Seal and Stamp
     D. Establish a Schedule
     E. Maintain Current Mailing Lists
     F. Prepare Mail for Automated Processing
     G. Reduce Mailing Costs
     H. Use Software Programs
     I. Use Internet Services
 VII. Incoming Mail
     A. Sort
     B. Open
     C. Keep Selected Envelopes
     D. Date and Time Stamp
     E. Read and Annotate
     F. Organize and Present
     G. Route
     H. Handle Mail When the Executive Is Out
VIII. Recycling
  IX. Future Mail Trends
   X. Summary
  XI. Key Terms
 XII. Professional Pointers
XIII. Office Procedures Reinforcement
XIV. Critical Thinking Activity
 XV. Office Applications
XVI. Online Research Application

TEACHING SUGGESTIONS

- If you work in a college or university that has a large mail department, make arrangements for your students to tour the facility and get an explanation of what type of equipment is used. If a tour is not possible, invite the manager of the area to explain the operation of the department to your students.
- Invite a representative from the USPS to explain projected future trends, the type of mail sorting equipment that is used, and to give tips on how organizations may cut their mail costs.

KEY TO SUPPLEMENTAL EXERCISE

A supplemental exercise is given on page 81 of the Applications Workbook. The student is to retrieve the mailing list that is on the student template disk, file SE13, and make the following changes to the list.

Montague Trading: Shantee Williams, Vice President
Klassen T. Industries: M. M. Nissen, CEO
The DuMundie Group; Robert Mosely, CEO

The student is then to sort the file by ZIP code, run a copy of the database, and print out mailing labels. The database and mailing labels are to be submitted to you.

Key to Database (with corrections)

Shantee Williams Vice President
Montague Trading
Suite 390C
Southfield MI 48034-0231

Alexander Watson CEO
International Laser Corporation
9490 Wade Hampton
Southfield MI 48034-1120

Alexander Yurishtopkof President
Glenn Mills Inc
1689 South Boulevard
Southfield MI 48037-1134

Kit Shaeffer President
Southern Trade Distributors
105 W Laurens Street
Southfield MI 48037-3421

Joan Centaria Vice President
International Marketing Group
2256 H Street NW
Detroit MI 48201-1144

Michel Bernstein CEO
Jepson & Bernstein
51 Highway East
Detroit MI 48201-1845

Floyd Grayson Director
Production Products
5521 Crossbeam Tower
Detroit MI 48202-3876

Christopher Bradbee President
Bradbee and Associates
668 North Telegraph Road
Detroit MI 48203-1256

Rolanda Jesus CEO
Broilhill Industries
Box 992 Forest Station
Detroit MI 48204-3366

Martha Leigh Director
The Vinsteed Company
12 Draw A
Detroit MI 48205-2920

Sheila Minor-Miller President
Kentuck Enterprises
PO Box 3651
Detroit MI 48205-7345

R Chambli Madlock President
Central Manufacturers Association
PO Box 8002
Detroit MI 48209-3423

Robert Mosely CEO
The DuMundie Group
8801 University Drive
Detroit MI 48210-7822

Kimara Kato President
Global Technologies Inc
779 Rose Lake Drive
Detroit MI 48211-7867

James Bowles President
Signal Corporation
Box 34144
Detroit MI 48217-2451

M M Nissen CEO
Klassen T Industries
Two Riverfront Plaza
Detroit MI 48221-4321

KEY TO OFFICE PROCEDURES REINFORCEMENT

1. Identify and describe the classifications of mail offered by the USPS.

   - Express Mail—Express mail is the fastest service available from the USPS. It is delivered 365 days a year. Items must weigh 70 pounds or less and measure 108 inches or less in combined length and girth.
   - Priority Mail—Priority Mail offers two-day service to most domestic destinations. Items must weigh 70 pounds or less and measure 108 inches in combined length and girth.
   - First-Class Mail—First-Class Mail includes letters, greeting cards, postcards, bills, and so forth. There is a charge for the first ounce on First-Class Mail and an additional charge for each ounce, plus an additional charge for nonstandard size dimensions.
   - Periodicals—Publishers and registered news agents are the only people who may mail publications at Periodicals rate.
   - Standard Mail (A)—Standard Mail (A) consists of mail weighing less than 16 ounces and is used primarily by retailers, catalogers, and other advertisers to promote products and services.
   - Standard Mail (B)—Standard Mail (B) is used for mailing items such as books, circulars, catalogs, and other printed matter and parcels that weigh 16 ounces or more.

- Parcel Post—Parcel Post consists of pieces exceeding 108 inches but not more than 130 inches in combined length and girth. Parcel Post is composed of four sub-classes—Parcel Post, Bound Printed Matter, Special Standard Mail, and Library Mail.

2. Identify and describe six mail services available from the USPS.

   The student may give any six of the following services.

   - Certificate of mailing provides evidence that the item has been mailed. There is a minimal charge for this service, and the certificate may be purchased at the time of mailing.
   - Registering mail provides maximum protection and security for valuable items. Registered mail is available only for First-Class Mail or Priority Mail.
   - Restricted delivery allows the mailer to send the item by direct delivery to the addressee or addressee's authorized agent only.
   - Return receipt is a service that provides a mailer with evidence of delivery.
   - Collect on delivery (COD) allows the mailer to collect the price of goods and/or postage on the items ordered by the addressee when they are delivered.
   - Certified mail provides a record of delivery for materials that have no monetary value.
   - Insured mail provides for coverage against loss or damage. Coverage may be obtained for up to $5,000.
   - Money orders may be obtained from the USPS. This service provides for safe transmission of money to individuals or institutions.
   - A mailer may fill out an Authorization to Hold Mail form that allows the post office to hold mail for a period of no more than 30 days.

3. Describe the responsibilities of an office professional for handling outgoing mail.

   The office professional has the following responsibilities when handling outgoing mail.

   - Checking enclosures
   - Preparing envelopes—addressing them properly and adhering to automation requirements
   - Sealing and stamping the mail
   - Establishing a schedule that meets the in-house or external pickup times
   - Maintaining current mailing lists
   - Preparing mail that adheres to the USPS Mail Classification Reform guidelines
   - Reducing mailing costs
   - Using software programs
   - Using Internet services

4. Describe the responsibilities of an office professional for handling incoming mail.

   The office professional has the following responsibilities when handling incoming mail.

   - Sorting
   - Opening
   - Keeping selected envelopes
   - Dating and time stamping
   - Reading and annotating
   - Organizing and presenting
   - Routing
   - Handling mail when the executive is out

5. List five projected mail trends.

   The student may list any five of the following trends.

   - Increased use of automation in processing mail
   - Increased use of the Internet to deliver mail services and software applications
   - Outsourcing
   - Increased technological improvements in mailroom equipment
   - Increased use of alternative delivery options in mail such as email and fax
   - Use of multifunctional equipment
   - Increased use of software that maintains mailing lists
   - Processing of incoming mail via computer imaging and integration of fax and email
   - Continual changes in the USPS
   - Increased market share for private mailers
   - Increased international partnerships
   - Continual training of mail personnel

KEY TO CRITICAL THINKING ACTIVITY

The student is given a case and asked to respond to these questions. Although the answers will vary, here are suggested responses.

1. Are there ethical considerations in this case? If so, what are they?

   Yes, there are ethical considerations. The first one—Eva should never use the company computer and company time to send personal messages. The second one—No one should be reading someone else's electronic mail.

2. Should Eva tell her supervisor about her job offer before the rumor spreads? Should Eva tell her supervisor that she communicates with her sister via company email?

   You owe your employer loyalty. If Eva has decided to take the job offer, she should tell her supervisor immediately. However, since there is a rumor, Eva should tell her supervisor about the offer and what she intends to do about it. Yes, Eva should tell her supervisor that she has sent personal email to her sister. She should explain that she will not do so in the future.

3. How can Eva learn if someone in her agency has access to her electronic mail? Should she file a complaint if she learns someone has been reading her email?

Eva should discuss the situation with her supervisor and ask if there is a way that other people within the organization can read email. She should explain that she has sent confidential company email, and she is concerned for the confidentially of that mail if someone else can read it. Eva should not file a complaint about her personal email; she was behaving unethically when she sent the mail.

4. Are there company policies that should be put in place as a result of this situation?

If there is no company policy stating that it is not acceptable to read someone else's email, a policy should be prepared. Also, the security of the email system should be checked. The policy also should remind employees that their passwords should never be given to someone else, they should not have someone else check their email, and they should never leave email on their screen with their password showing when they are away from their desk.

KEY TO OFFICE APPLICATIONS

OA13-1 (Goals 1 and 2)

Correspondence	Service Used	Mail Classification and/or Service
Letter to client in France	Private service for delivery the next day	International Priority
Book weighing 18 ounces	USPS	Standard Mail (B)
Contract with a new client; proof that the contract is received is needed	USPS	First-Class, Return receipt
Check for $250 for AMA dues	USPS	First-Class
Report that must reach Paris tomorrow	Private service for delivery the next day	International Priority
Contract that must reach New York by 10 a.m.	USPS or private service	Express Mail (check with USPS to see if it will get there by 10 a.m.; if not, use a private service; also check cost of each service)
A letter that must reach California within two days	USPS	Priority Mail
Note to recently promoted Vice President in Germany	USPS	International Mail—letters/letter packages
Memo that must reach Paris within 30 minutes	Fax	

OA13-2 (Goal 2)

The student is to prepare a fax, using the fax cover sheet that is on the student template disk. Here is possible wording for the fax.

TO: Avion LeFever
FROM: Student's name
DATE: Current date
SUBJ: Arrival of Juan Menendez

Juan Menendez will be arriving in Paris on American Airlines, Flight 750, Tuesday, April 23, at 8:15 a.m. Please have someone pick him up at the airport and take him to the Paris office. Let me know by 3 p.m. this afternoon the name of the person who will be picking him up. Thanks.

OA13-3 (Goal 3)

The student is to sort the mail given on student template disk in file OA13-3, using the form provided. Also, two letters appearing on pages 79 and 80 of the Applications Workbook are to be annotated.

Type of Mail	Priority Order
Letter marked "confidential"	To be placed to one side and given to Mr. Menendez—not sorted
Package marked "personal"	To be placed to one side and given to Mr. Menendez—not sorted
Fax	Immediate action folder
Envelope marked "Priority Mail"	Immediate action folder
Envelope marked "Express Mail"	Immediate action folder
A certified letter	Immediate action folder
Letter from a client	Immediate action folder
Statement from a consultant	Routine correspondence
Interoffice memo	Routine correspondence
Annual report for Hanover Bank	Routine correspondence
Current edition of *Fortune*	Informational mail
Sales catalog	Information mail

OA13-3 (Goal 3)

The student is to select three classmates to work with on the project. Using the Internet, the students are to research services provided by the following mail and shipping services:

- USPS
- Western Union
- FedEx
- UPS

A report is to be prepared and submitted to you.

KEY TO ONLINE RESEARCH APPLICATION

ORA13-4 (Goal 4)

The student is to select three classmates to work with on this project. Using the Internet, the students are to research the services provided by the following mail and shipping services:

- USPS
- Western Union
- FedEx
- UPS

A report of the findings is to be prepared and submitted to you.

KEY TO END OF PART 3 ACTIVITIES

Vocabulary Review: Part 3 (Chapters 9–13)

If you are grading these items, each one is worth two points.

1. communication
2. self-concept
3. verbal communication
4. encoding
5. territoriality
6. parallelism
7. passive voice
8. readability
9. emoticon
10. you approach
11. block and modified block
12. open and mixed punctuation
13. documentation
14. analogy
15. Express Mail
16. First-Class Mail
17. registered mail
18. electronic mail
19. annotating
20. OCR and BCS (bar code sorter)
21. telecommunications
22. local area
23. Centrex
24. unified messaging
25. Wide Area Telecommunications Service (WATS)

Language Skills Practice: Part 3 (Chapters 9–13)

If you are grading these items, each one (including the word division rules) is worth two points.

1. The program starts at 8:45 a.m. on Wednesday, March 25.
2. The building is located on Azalea Boulevard.
3. The Honorable Susan Baynes Harris will speak at the meeting.
4. We have planned trips to the Northeast and Southwest this summer and fall.
5. She is an office assistant for the Business Division of Chesapeake Community College.
6. Her daughter is almost 16.
7. Approximately 20 people are in my class, and 15 of them were in my last class.
8. In military correspondence, dates are written in this manner: 15 November 2001.
9. There was a disagreement among the team's members.
10. Pam feels bad today.
11. Everyone in the room knows that Austin is the capital of Texas.
12. That is a capital idea!
13. When the lawsuit is tried, our counsel is planning to cite several recent court decisions.
14. The two secretaries' raucous laughter disturbed the other employees in the office.
15. The women's coats were checked in the lobby of the building.
16. People, materials, and production are three essential components of any organization.
17. The salesperson said, "Show the client how using the computer will save the company money."
18. Fill in the form, put it in the envelope (it is stamped and addressed), and mail it today.
19. Having traveled throughout Europe and the Middle East on numerous occasions, he was considered a world traveler.
20. Potatoes are a common vegetable and can be used in a variety of dishes.
21. There are three attorneys who have offices in this building.
22. Self-satisfied
    Rule: Divide hyphenated compound words at existing hyphens only.
23. gradu-ation
    Rule: If two one-letter syllables occur together within a word, divide between the one-letter syllables.

PART 4: RECORDS MANAGEMENT

CHAPTER 14

RULES AND PROCEDURES

The office professional has primary responsibility in managing and maintaining records, whether these records are paper, electronic, or microimage. Since paper records continue to be maintained in abundance in most office (with a projected 60 percent of all record storage in 2000 being a manual or paper system), the student is introduced to records management rules and procedures through manual system examples. This chapter will help the student become familiar with the basics of records management, including learning the filing rules and how to use alphabetic, numeric, subject, and geographic methods of storage.

STUDENT GOALS

1. Learn and use filing rules.
2. Identify and use the four basic storage methods.
3. Determine the types of paper storage equipment available.

CHAPTER OUTLINE

I. Introduction
II. Your Goals
III. The Importance of Records Management
IV. Alphabetic Indexing Rules
  A. Rule 1: Indexing Order of Units
  B. Rule 2: Minor Words and Symbols in Business Names
  C. Rule 3: Punctuation and Possessives
  D. Rule 4: Personal Names
  E. Rule 5: Titles and Suffixes
  F. Rule 6: Prefixes—Articles and Particles
  G. Rule 7: Numbers in Business Names
  H. Rule 8: Organizations and Institutions
  I. Rule 9: Identical Names
  J. Rule 10: Government Names
V. Indexing Rules for Computer Applications
  A. Computer Filing Considerations
  B. Computer Sorting

VI. Storage Methods
  A. Alphabetic Storage Method
    1. Alphabetic Storage Advantages
    2. Alphabetic Storage Disadvantages
  B. Subject Storage Method
    1. Subject Storage Advantages
    2. Subject Storage Disadvantages
  C. Numeric Storage Method
    1. Basic Parts
    2. Storage Procedure
    3. Numeric Storage Advantages
    4. Numeric Storage Disadvantages
    5. Variations of Numeric Storage
  D. Geographic Method
    1. Geographic Storage Advantages
    2. Geographic Storage Disadvantages
VII. Storing Procedures
  A. Inspect
  B. Index
    1. Incoming Letters
    2. Outgoing Letters
  C. Code
  D. Cross-Reference
  E. Sort
  F. Store
VIII. Manual Records Retrieval, Retention, Transfer, and Disposal
  A. Records Retrieval
    1. Requisition Form
    2. Out Guide and Out Folder
  B. Records Retention
    1. Vital Records
    2. Important Records
    3. Useful Records
    4. Nonessential Records
  C. Records Transfer
    1. Perpetual Transfer
    2. Periodic Transfer
  D. Records Disposal

TEACHING SUGGESTIONS

- Invite the Registrar from your institution to discuss how student records are managed, from the point of origination to the storage process.
- Invite a records manager from a large company to discuss the records management systems used.

KEY TO SUPPLEMENTAL EXERCISE

A Supplemental Exercise is provided in the Applications Workbook on page 93. The student is to design a requisition form for charging out files and use the form to complete a requisition for four situations given. Although the forms will vary, suggested solutions are given here.

RECORDS REQUEST

NAME ON RECORD Del Norte Lock Co.   DATE OF RECORD 9-20-2001
SUBJECT Vault Servicing
DATE TAKEN 10-1-2001   DATE TO BE RETURNED 10-9-2001
REQUESTER Edward Robinson   DEPARTMENT Acctg.

RECORDS REQUEST

NAME ON RECORD De Kalb Jewelers   DATE OF RECORD 9-14-2001
SUBJECT Price Quotation
DATE TAKEN 11-15-2001   DATE TO BE RETURNED 11-22-2001
REQUESTER Katherine Malcolm   DEPARTMENT Acctg.

RECORDS REQUEST

NAME ON RECORD Karla Nikimoto   DATE ON RECORD 11-1-2001
SUBJECT Reorganization
DATE TAKEN 11-29-2001   DATE TO BE RETURNED 12-5-2001
REQUESTER Jada Bartlett   DEPARTMENT Human Resources

RECORDS REQUEST

NAME ON RECORD AD Ford   DATE ON RECORD 11-24-2001
SUBJECT Bankruptcy
DATE TAKEN 12-2-2001   DATE TO BE RETURNED 12-10-2001
REQUESTER John Anders   DEPARTMENT Acctg

Note: Student will use current year; the year is shown here merely as an example.

KEY TO OFFICE PROCEDURES REINFORCEMENT

1. Define records management and describe the value of records to a business.

   Records management is the systematic control of records over the record life cycle, which is from the creation of the record to its final disposition.

   The value of records to business includes:

   - History for the business
   - Information contained in records may be used to make decisions and to plan for the future
   - Legal value by providing evidence of business transactions such as articles of incorporation, real estate transactions, and contracts
   - Financial value through records needed in audits and for tax purposes
   - Personnel value through such items as employment applications, date of hire, evaluations of employees, payroll records, and employment termination records
   - Day-to-day operational value through such records as policy and procedures manuals, organization charts, minutes of meetings, information sent to clients and customers, and sales reports

2. List the advantages and disadvantages of the alphabetic and numeric storage methods.

   Advantages of an alphabetic system are:

   - It is a direct access system. There is no need to refer to anything except the file to find the name.
   - The dictionary order of arrangement is simple to understand.
   - Misfiling is easily checked by alphabetic sequence.
   - It may be less costly to operate than other filing methods because of direct access.
   - Only one sorting is necessary.
   - Papers relating to one originator are filed in the same location.

   Disadvantages of an alphabetic system are:

   - Misfiling may result when rules are not followed.
   - Similarly spelled names may cause confusion when filed under the alphabetic method.
   - Related records may be filed in more than one place.
   - Expansion may create problems. This statement is especially true if the expansion takes place in a section of the file where there is no room remaining for the insertion of more guides and folders.
   - Excessive cross-referencing can congest the files.
   - Confidentiality of the files cannot be maintained since the file folders bearing names are instantly seen by anyone who happens to glance at a folder.

Advantages of a numeric system are:

- Expansion is unlimited.
- It is confidential. A card file must be consulted before files on important papers can be located.
- Once an index card is prepared and a number is assigned to a record, filing by number is quicker than filing alphabetically.
- Misfiled folders are easily located because numbers out of place are easier to locate than misfiled alphabetic records.

Disadvantages of a numeric system:

- It is an indirect method. The card file must be consulted before a paper can be filed.
- More equipment is necessary; therefore, the cost is higher.

3. Describe the steps in proper storage procedures.

   - Inspect
   - Index
   - Code
   - Cross-reference
   - Sort
   - Store

4. Name and briefly describe the four categories into which records can be classified.

   The four categories into which records can be classified are:

   - Vital records—Records that cannot be replaced and must never be destroyed.
   - Important records—Those records that can only be replaced with considerable time and cost; may be transferred to inactive storage but not destroyed.
   - Useful records—Represent the operation of the organization; may be moved to inactive storage or destroyed after a certain period of time.
   - Nonessential records—Have no future value; should be destroyed after they serve the purpose for which they were created.

5. List at least six tips to use in locating misplaced or lost files.

   The student may list any 6 of the following 12 tips:

   - Look at the folder just before and after the correct folder.
   - Search between folders.
   - Look in the GENERAL file.
   - Determine if a file or document slipped to the bottom of the drawer.
   - Carefully review every document in a folder in case chronological order may not have been used.
   - Look under the second, third, or remaining units of a name if it is not under the first unit.

- Look at closely related letters or numbers; for example, C for G or K for H.
- Check under different spellings of names.
- Check for transposed numbers.
- Look in a related subject file.
- Check in the "to be filed" basket.
- Search your desk and your employer's desk.

KEY TO CRITICAL THINKING ACTIVITY

The student is given a case and asked to respond to the following items. Although the answers to the questions will vary, a suggested response is given here.

- What advice would you give Ms. Townes for handling the situation?
- Prepare a suggested plan of action to give to the vice president.

The student is asked to discuss his or her suggestions with the class.

- What advice would you give Ms. Townes for handling the situation?

Ms. Townes has reason to "suspect" Franklin. However, all evidence is circumstantial. She has no proof of anything. Franklin has been an outstanding employee; or at least, she has believed he has been. His performance appraisals have been excellent. She should tell the vice president that she wants to discuss the matter with the company attorney since there are numerous legal implications. If Franklin is involved, she needs to handle the matter carefully; a wrong step here could cost the company a lawsuit. (The vice president should check with the salesperson's supervisor to see if he or she is aware of any confidential information being taken by the salesperson.)

- Prepare a plan of action to give to the vice president.

The plan of action should include the following steps:

— Ask to discuss the matter with the company attorney.
— Call Franklin in and ask him what files he was giving to the salesperson. Follow the discussion with Franklin with a written memo of what was said. If Franklin offers some reason for giving the files to the individual, record the information. If Franklin is not cooperative and refuses to answer, the company attorney needs to be informed immediately. (Failure to respond in such a situation is serious; the company may want to put Franklin on suspension from his job until more is discovered about the situation. Ms. Townes should discuss suspension with the vice president before acting.)
— Depending on Franklin's response, call in the other employees on an individual basis and ask them if they have any information about files leaving the office without being recorded. (Ms. Townes should not use Franklin's name or tell the other employees about the incident.)
— Establish a temporary system in which no files leave the office without the signature of Ms. Townes. Put out a memo to the entire company about the new procedure.
— Do not ask Franklin to work overtime for the present.
— Monitor all employees carefully.

(Note: Whatever the students' responses, it should be pointed out that the situation should be checked out carefully with legal counsel. It is a serious matter. Not only are files leaving the office, but upper management has reason to believe that confidential information is being leaked to a competitor.)

KEY TO OFFICE APPLICATIONS

OA14-1 (Goals 1 and 2)

The student is to prepare names for a geographic file from the student template disk in the file OA14-1.

Atlanta	Georgia	C	C	Pryor	Printing	
Atlanta	Georgia	Colonial	Store	The		
Atlanta	Georgia	US	Aluminum	Inc		
Atlanta	Georgia	V	and	R	Services	
Atlanta	Georgia	V	I	E	Data	Services
Atlanta	Georgia	Vandys				
Atlanta	Georgia	VanGuard	Corporation			
Atlanta	Georgia	Vasek	Finewood	Inc		
Atlanta	Georgia	VIP	Builders			
Atlanta	Georgia	VS	Café			
Detroit	Michigan	Committee	for	Pollution	Control	
Detroit	Michigan	Fassallo	and	Ashmore	PC	
Detroit	Michigan	Commuters	Snack	Bar		
Detroit	Michigan	PryorLee				
Detroit	Michigan	Pryors				
New York City	New York	Colonial	Crafts			
New York City	New York	Eureka	Equipment	Co		
New York City	New York	Fairacres	Dairy			
New York City	New York	Father	Flanagan			
New York City	New York	Grant	E	E		
New York City	New York	Health	Department			
New York City	New York	Moores	Building	Supply		
New York City	New York	Samuel	Moore	Corp		
New York City	New York	Severn	Brothers			
New York City	New York	Severn	Stella	Inc		
New York City	New York	Street	Florist	The		
New York City	New York	VCP	Vacuum	Cleaner	Products	
New York City	New York	VIP	Builders			
Southfield	Michigan	Donna	Vaughan	and	Associates	
Southfield	Michigan	Ulysses	E	Aiken	Corp	

OA14-2 (Goals 1 and 2)

The student is to prepare names for a numeric file, with the first number being 100. (Numbers are assigned in the order in which records are received; the student is to assign numbers in the order in which the names are listed in the Applications Workbook, with the first name, *Grant's Drum City,* assigned 100: the second name, *Lee Gray and Company,* assigned 101: etc.) The names are given in the list of clients in the Applications Workbook on page 89. After the numbers are assigned, the student is to prepare 3 × 5 cards for the card file by listing the clients' names in indexing order and placing the appropriate number on the card. The cards are to be arranged in alphabetical order and submitted to you.

102	Andy	Grantella	Tuneup	Masters	
119	Boyce	Graham	Photography		
107	Earl	Greenlee	Custom	Drapery	
120	Graham	Marie	M	Ms	
121	Grainger	Wilma	Ms		
123	Grand	Avenue	Clinic		
124	Grand	Bancshares	Inc		
103	Grand	Prairie	Self	Storage	
122	Grandbury	State	Bank		
125	Grandstaff	J	W	Jr	
126	Grandstaff	J	W	Sr	
100	Grants	Drum	City		
131	Graphic	Finishers			
128	Grattafiori	Cecil	II		
129	Grattafiori	Cecil	III		
127	Grattafiori	Corporation			
130	Graveley	Hardware			
132	Gray	Maintenance	Contractors		
136	GrayCollin	Electric			
135	Grays	Diesel			
137	Grays	Nursery			
108	Great	American	Coverup		
109	Great	China	Restaurant		
110	Greater	Mount	Olive	Baptist	Church
111	Green	Bay	Packaging		
105	Green	Tree	Apartments		
106	Greenfields	Inc			
104	Greentree	Pharmacy			
112	Guaranty	Bank			
113	Gulf	American	Products		
114	Gulf	Fire	Sprinklers	Inc	
116	Gurkoff	Jerry			
115	Gutierrez	Jose			
118	Gyo	Ha	Industrial	Co	
117	Gypsi	Enterprises	Inc		
101	Lee	Gray	and	Company	
134	Tom	Gray	Paint	Company	
133	Veo	Gray	Realtor		

OA14-3 (Goals 1 and 2)

The student is to create a database and enter the records of clients from Job 14-1. The field for the states is to be changed to the two-letter state abbreviation. Several records, listed in the Applications Workbook on page 90, need to be added to the list. The records are to be sorted by clients' names, and a copy printed and submitted to you.

C	C	Pryor	Printing	Atlanta	GA	30314
Colonial	Crafts			New York City	NY	10056
Colonial	Store	The		Atlanta	GA	30312
Committee	for	Pollution	Control	Detroit	MI	48217
Commuters	Snack	Bar		Detroit	MI	48211
Donna	Vaughan	and	Associates	Southfield	MI	48034
Eureka	Equipment	Co		New York City	NY	10023
Fairacres	Dairy			New York City	NY	10028
Fassallo	and	Ashmore	PC	Detroit	MI	48215
Father	Flanagan	Ashmore		New York City	NY	10023
Grant	E	E		New York City	NY	10079
Haley	Corporation			Detroit	MI	48219
Moore	Samuel			New York City	NY	10078
Moores	Building	Supply		New York City	NY	10078
Mountain	Rafters			Detroit	MI	48216
New	York	City	Health (4th unit) Department (5th unit)	New York City	NY	10045
Outfitters	Inc			Detroit	MI	48220
PryorLee				Detroit	MI	48217
Pryos				Detroit	MI	48201
Severn	Bros			New York City	NY	10056
Severn	Stella			New York City	NY	10002
Street	Florist	The		New York City	NY	10066
Ulysses	E	Aiken	Corporation	Southfield	MI	48034
US	Aluminum	Inc		Atlanta	A	20201
V	and	R	Services	Atlanta	GA	30311
V	I	E	Data (4th unit) Services (5th unit)	Atlanta	GA	30311
Vandys				Atlanta	GA	30307
VanGuard	Corporation			Atlanta	GA	30307
Vasek	Finewood	Inc		Atlanta	GA	30303
VCP	Vacuum	Cleaner	Products	New York City	NY	10021
VIP	Builders			Atlanta	GA	30324
VIP	Builders			New York	NY	10024
VS	Café			Atlanta	GA	30310

OA14-4 (Goals 1 and 2)

The student is asked to print out four letters and two memo-randums from the student template disk, index, code, and sort the correspondence in preparation for filing in a subject file; the student is to prepare a cross-reference sheet on the letter to Malcolm Holms. Suggested coding is as follows:

Letter to J.T. Fernandez—Community
Letter to Paula Cronk—Software
Letter to Fran Staples—Training
Letter to Malcolm Holms—Customers—Paris
    (cross-reference—Customers—Frankford)
Memo to Flex Blanchard, Todd Atkinson, Hazel
    Morrow—Budget
Memo to Donald Stringfellow—Budget

OA14-5 (Goals 1 and 2)

The student is to refer to file OA14-5 on the student template disk. This file is to be merged with the names on page 92 of the Applications Workbook in alphabetical order. A copy is to be printed and submitted to you. The merged file is given here.

A W Franklin Paint and Body
Allen Erbs Plant Shop
Brother Ford
Brother Fords Candy Shop
Cecilia Ford Development Corporation
D G Motors
DeKalb Jewelers
DelNorte Lock Company
DeVille Marie R Dr
DFore M R
Doctor Erbs Shop
Dorio Vaudreuill Construction
Down Town Merchants
11 Stop Club The
11 Street Coiffures
E and E Record Company
East West Airport
Eat More Burger Company
Eighth Street Drug
El Most Productions
El Taquito Café
El Tec Sales Inc
Elva Cars Dallas
Ely Company The
Enchiladas Restaurant Cantina
Enclave at Valley Ranch The
Equitable Savings Association
Erles Exxon Station
Erma and Fays Beauty Shop
Ernest Allen Chevrolet
Ernies Grocery and Market
Ernst and Ernst Accountants
EZ Cleaning Service
4 Avenue Garage
4 by 4 Lumber Company
4 Entertainers The
4 L Plumbing
4 M Construction
Father Michael
Ford A D
Ford A F
Ford A J Jr

Ford A J Sr
Ford Andrew Sr
Ford Ann D
Ford Brothers Motor
Ford Edsel O
Ford Georgia Mrs
Ford Harriett W
Ford Virgil Rev
Ford William T
FordClark A L
FordClark Anita Lee
Forde Georgia E
ForeAft Winetta
Foree James
Foretich Chung (may be cross-referenced under "Chung Foretich")
Foretich Chung Mrs (may be cross-referenced under "Chung Foretich")
Forfang T E
Forfang Ty
Forney and Forquet International Inc
Forty Cleaners
Four Acres The
Four Seasons Hotel
Frazier R T (Gainesville)
Frazier R T (Jacksonville)
Freeds Studio
FROX Radio Station
Gertrude Erier Real Estate
Lee Ford Dry Goods Store
New Castle Pen Shop
New York Pharmacy
Roger R. Ford Credit
Ruth Ford Barbeque
T A Fore Realty

KEY TO ONLINE RESEARCH APPLICATION

ORA14-6 (Goal 3)

The student is to use the Internet to research the following:

• Types of manual storage equipment available
• Types of information available from ARMA

The student is to prepare a short synopsis of his or her findings, listing the sources used. A copy is to be submitted to you.

CHAPTER 15

RECORDS MANAGEMENT TECHNOLOGY

The electronic storage and retrieval of records is presented in this chapter. Students are instructed in the use of electronic and microimage systems and are provided examples of the integration of computer and microimage systems. Trends in records management are briefly discussed.

STUDENT GOALS

1. Describe and use electronic and microimage systems.
2. Identify examples of the integration of computer and microimage systems.
3. Explain future trends in records management.

CHAPTER OUTLINE

I. Introduction
II. Your Goals
III. Information Management Systems
   A. Electronic Database Systems
      1. Database Software
      2. Decentralized and Centralized
      3. Storage and Retrieval
      4. Safety and Security
         a. Safety
         b. Security
   B. Document Management Systems
      1. Document Management Software
      2. Digital Archiving
      3. Storage Methods
         a. Compact Disks (CDs)
         b. Digital Versatile Disks (DVDs)
      4. Advantages of Document Management Systems
   C. Microimage Systems
      1. Microforms
         a. Microfilm
         b. Microfiche
      2. System Elements
         a. Converting to Film
         b. Processing
         c. Duplicating
         d. Displaying and Reproducing
         e. Storing
      3. Legal Aspects
      4. Evaluation of Micrographic Systems

   D. Integration of Electronic and Microimage Systems
      1. Computer-Output Microfilm (COM)
      2. Computer-Input Microfilm (CIM)
      3. Computer-Aided Retrieval (CAR)
      4. Integration of Fax and Micrographics
      5. Benefits of the Integration of Electronic and Microimage Systems
   E. Computer Output to Laser Disk (COLD) Systems
      1. Storage Process
      2. Storage Methods
      3. Advantages of COLD technology
   F. Records Migration
IV. Trends in Records Management
V. Summary
VI. Key Terms
VII. Professional Pointers
VIII. Office Procedures Reinforcement
IX. Critical Thinking Activity
X. Office Applications
XI. Online Research Application

TEACHING SUGGESTIONS

- Consult with the records/personnel/archives office at your school. Ask them if your class can visit the office and learn about the types of technology that are used to retain student and/or employee information. Ask the individual to demonstrate some of the technology for the class.
- Ask the students to visit the school library or local library and give a report on the types of technology used in storing information in a library setting. You may want to take the class to the library as a field trip and have someone from the library demonstrate the different types of technologies and how they are used.
- Ask the students to visit the local historical society and find out how they deal with records storage. Since the goal of this organization is archival storage, students may learn about different kinds of technologies that they have not been exposed to in this chapter.

KEY TO SUPPLEMENTAL EXERCISE

An additional office application is provided in the Applications Workbook on pages 100 and 101. For this exercise, the student is to categorize document names from a listing of stored information. The student should determine which of the five subdirectories should be used to store the informa-

tion. Students are to write the name of the appropriate subdirectory next to the document name. The solution should be as follows:

```
         12-05-01                              Directory C:\My Documents\*.*
         Free:   23,078,554

                     .           Current  <Dir>
General    ACCTG          .               4,951     03-29-00    04:40P
General    CPED           .              28,789     05-26-00    03:15P
Travel     ITIN           .TRA            3,334     05-04-00    09:50A
          ┌L-JTFER        .LVP            6,452     05-05-00    08:58A
          │ L-GROVES       .               3,101     07-30-00    10:14A
          │ L-RLCAR        .LVP            8,775     05-09-00    02:45P
          │ L-TRANSL       .              13,498     04-11-00    10:23A
          │ M-ACCTG        .               9,678     07-13-00    02:30P
Correspondence│ M-BUDGET   .LVP            7,933     05-12-00    09:33A
          │ M-EDPR         .              15,654     01-19-00    07:45A
          │ M-PLAN         .               3,590     05-22-00    08:55A
          │ M-SPACE        .               2,554     06-14-00    11:39A
          │ M-VDOT         .              10,324     11-03-00    12:10P
          └M-WARNE         .               8,101     04-22-00    04:12P
General    STAPLES        .               7,437     06-12-00    12:05P
          ┌TRANSPO        .TRA            7,221     06-06-00    11:45A
Travel     │ TRIP1         .TEX           12,090     05-24-00    09:11A
          │ TRIP2          .COL            8,945     08-10-00    01:22P
          └TRIP3           .ALA            9,987     10-05-00    02:50P
General    VAPERS         .              28,642     09-17-00    10:12A

         12-05-01                          Directory C:\My Documents\LVP\*.*
         Free:   21,789,020

                     .           Current  <Dir>
General    ANNE           .               9,459     04-15-00    08:28A
General    ANNEVAL        .              12,978     02-04-00    02:01P
General    ASTOR          .               3,907     06-08-00    05:15P
General    BIO-SHOR       .               5,087     07-28-00    08:29A
General    BIO43          .              10,312     07-30-00    10:39A
Forms      BUDGET         .FOR            8,740     08-19-00    11:04A
General    D-PROP         .SUM            6,398     05-12-00    01:46P
General    DIRECT         .              38,451     04-22-00    03:49P



Education


General    EL-MINS        .               8,391     07-16-00    09:38A
General    JOBDESC        .              10,329     05-28-00    11:34A
General    FI-PROOF       .               3,290     02-12-00    08:37A
          ┌L-ATLEE        .               2,556     03-16-00    09:58A
          │ L-PAPER        .               4,489     04-06-00    01:19P
          │ L-PTA          .               3,833     05-17-00    04:59P
Correspondence│ L-RESUME   .               7,911     10-19-00    04:22P
          │ L-SCHOL        .              10,047     11-21-00    07:59A
          │ M-DSTRIP       .LVP            2,558     05-12-00    09:59A
          │ M-LEAVE        .               3,975     11-30-00    04:45P
          └M-PROMO         .               9,226     05-09-00    11:27A
Travel     MILEAGE        .TRA           12,534     02-27-00    10:48A
Forms      PROOF          .FOR           29,756     04-25-00    03:15P
General    ROD-BIO        .               6,799     06-11-00    09:14A
Forms      RCC            .FOR           31,224     07-24-00    01:57P
General    SCH-CU         .FOR            2,997     08-26-00    02:46P
Forms      TRAVEL         .FOR           24,513     10-13-00    04:10P
```

KEY TO OFFICE PROCEDURES REINFORCEMENT

1. Describe the four parts of an information management system.

   The four parts of an information management system are inputting data, processing the data through integration with other data, outputting the data, and storing and retrieving the data.

2. Describe the differences in a decentralized and a centralized electronic storage system.

   In a decentralized storage system, records are accessible only on the disk or the tape to which they were saved. A centralized system links the access of data through local area networks (LANs) or wide-area networks (WANs) so that many individuals and/or locations have access.

3. List the advantages associated with document management software.

   Some of the features of a document management software system include the ability to:

   - Log in documents
   - Print file labels
   - Track active files, inactive files, vital records, and off-premise storage
   - Provide an inventory of all records

- Follow up on overdue files
- Track nonpaper documents, such as disks and micro-forms
- Generate activity reports by department and user
- Generate records retention and disposal guidelines

4. Describe the computer-micrographics technologies called COM, CIM, and CAR.
   a. COM is computer-output microfilm. This technology produces computer documents directly on microforms instead of on paper printouts.
   b. CIM is computer-input microfilm. This technology works in the reverse of COM. Digital information is translated from microfilm storage into computer-readable data for use on the computer.
   c. CAR is computer-aided retrieval. This system provides assistance in the retrieval of randomly stored microforms. All documents are assigned an identifier and are indexed on a computer system. A user can then search the index to locate documents from a specific author or in a particular subject.

5. Explain why COLD technology is important and advantageous as a storage system.

COLD technology takes report files and rewrites them onto magnetic or optical disks in a special format, which can be redisplayed to a variety of system users. With COLD technology, the information is copied to a storage media but remains accessible to authorized users on the system. This gives users instant access to information. COLD technology brings us closer to the "paperless office" since the printing, copying, and filing steps of the COM system are eliminated.

Advantages of COLD technology include:

- Instant access to information and elimination of the cumbersome and time-consuming tasks associated with microform retrieval.
- Elimination of costs associated with microfilm production, distribution, and retrieval.
- Instant access in branch offices or remote sites to current COLD data through network storage instead of having to duplicate and distribute microfilm reports.
- Increased storage capacity. Since most systems come with compression technology, you can store 50 percent more information on your chosen storage medium.
- Confidentiality of information is controlled through normal information systems security instead of the physical security necessary for paper and microform records.

KEY TO CRITICAL THINKING ACTIVITY

1. If Karla knows that the file clerk who resigned is a good employee, she should talk with the person about staying with the company. It is expensive to train new employees, and productivity suffers when a competent employee leaves. However, if the file clerk who resigned is incompetent, Karla should accept the resignation. Karla should work with the two file clerks who were noncommittal at the meeting to help them improve their performance. She should also use their help in attempting to win the cooperation of the other two defensive file clerks.

2. Karla should consider the following suggestions when reviewing the situation:
   a. Karla should have called the employees together to get their ideas about why procedures were handled in a certain way and how improvements could be made.
   b. Inefficient procedures are likely the source of the problem rather than the employees' unwillingness to do their job well. Karla should lead an effort to analyze records management procedures for efficiency. Procedures that are unnecessary should be discarded, and procedures that are determined to be necessary should be improved.
   c. Karla should set clear standards for the employees' job performance. A records management procedures manual would aid in establishing responsibilities for the personnel.
   d. A hasty confrontation with accusations is never the best approach to solving problems. As a records manager, Karla should foster an atmosphere of cooperation in which the employees would want to establish a model records center.

KEY TO OFFICE APPLICATIONS

OA15-1 (Goal 1)

The draft of a records retention and disposition schedule is provided on the student template disk. Students are to make the revisions noted on the hard copy in their Applications Workbook. The revisions call for deleted material to be shown by using the "strikethrough" feature, and new material should be underlined. A copy with the marked revisions should be noted as Draft 2. A sample copy is shown on the following page.

Provide your students with the following information to be used; this information does not appear on the disk. Forgive us for this inconvenience; the disk will be revised on the second printing of the textbook.

DRISCOLL & CLINE
Records Retention and Disposition Schedule

This schedule is continuing authority for the retention and disposition of the records as stated and supersedes previously approved applicable schedules.

Record Category/Title	Scheduled Retention and Disposition
1. Acknowledgment File	Destroy 3 months after acnowledgment and referral
2. Administrative Files See Correspondence Records	
3. Board/Conference/CommitteeMeeting Records	
a. Records relating to executive establishment, organization, membership, and policy	Retain 3 years for administrative use; purge all material of non-enduring value and/or microfilm according to standards
b. Records created by agenda, minutes, final reports, and related records documenting the accomplishment of official boards	Retain 3 years for administrative use; purge all material of non-enduring value and/or microfilm according to standards
4. Correspondence Records	
a. Correspondence/subject files of executive officers not duplicated elsewhere that document establishment of policies, procedures, and achievements	Retain 3 years for administrative use; purge all material of non-enduring value and/or microfilm according to standards
b. General correspondence: Letters of inquiry, informative or suggestive in nature, which address specific issues, projects, or cases	Retain same as 4 a.
c. Administrative files: Inquiries, responses, letters, and other miscellaneous correspondence	Retain same as 4 a.
5. Environmental Impact Files	Permanent
6. Publications: Pamphlets, reports, brochures, published or processed	Retain until superseded, and then transfer one copy to the archive files
7. Reference Files	Review annually; remove and destroy all nonessential material
8. Records Management Records	Permanent until superseded or revised
Records that relate to the management of records, including such matters as forms, correspondence, reports, mail, and files management; the use of microforms, work processing, vital records programs; and all other aspects of records management not covered elsewhere in this schedule	

OA15-1 (CONTINUED)

DRISCOLL & CLINE
Records Retention and Disposition Schedule

This schedule is continuing authority for the retention and disposition of the records as stated and supersedes previously approved applicable schedules.

Record Category/Title	Scheduled Retention and Disposition
1. Acknowledgment File	Destroy 3 months after acknowledgment and referral
2. Administrative Databases See Electronic Records	
3. Administrative Files See Correspondence Records	
4. Board/Conference/Committee Meeting Records	
a. Records pertaining to executive establishment, organization, membership, and policy	Retain 3 years for administrative use; purge all material of non-enduring value and/or microfilm according to standards
b. Records created by agenda, minutes, final reports, and related records documenting the accomplishments of official boards	Retain same as 4 a.
5. Correspondence Records	
a. Correspondence/subject files of executive officers not duplicated elsewhere that document establishment of policies, procedures, and achievements	Retain same as 4 a.

OA15-1

RECORDS RETENTION

AND

DISPOSITION

OA15-1 (CONTINUED)

b. Letters of inquiry, which address specific issues, projects, or cases or refer to corporate operations	Retain same as 4 a.
c. Inquiries, responses, letters and other miscellaneous correspondence generated in the course of daily business	Retain same as 4 a.
6. Electronic Mail/FAX Documents	Retain with related files or records and follow established retention and disposition for that file or record
7. Electronic Records	
a. Created solely to test system performance, such as test records, as well as documentation for the electronic files/records	Delete/destroy when no longer needed
b. Used to create or update a master file, including but not limited to, work files, valid transaction files, and intermediate input/output records	Delete after information has been transferred to the master file and verified
c. Serve to replace, in whole or part, administrative records schedule for disposal under one or more items in the General Schedule	Delete after the expiration of the retention period authorized for the disposable hard copy file or when no longer needed, whichever is later
d. Serve as administrative databases that support administrative functions	Destroy or delete when superseded or obsolete or upon authorized destruction of related master file or database

OA15-1 (CONTINUED)

e. Created as word processing files, such as letters, messages, memoranda, reports, policies, and manuals recorded on hard or floppy diskettes	Delete when no longer needed to create a hard copy
8. Environmental Impact Files	Permanent
9. Publications, Pamphlets, reports, brochures, manuals, and other published or processed documents	Retain until superseded and then transfer 1 copy to the archives
10. Reference Files	Review annually; remove and destroy all nonessential material
11. Records Management Documents that relate to the management of records, including such documents as forms, correspondence, reports, mail, and files management; the use of microforms, word processing, vital records; and all other aspects of records management not covered elsewhere in this schedule	Permanent until superseded or revised

OA15-2 (Goal 1)

Students are to create a database that includes information regarding all employees in the Records and Information Systems Department. Employees completed the forms that are found on pages 98–99 in the Applications Workbook. All information from the forms should be incorporated in the database structure. A sample copy of a database table is shown below.

Employees

Employee #	Last	First	MI	Address	Address 2	City	State
1735-7869	Johnson	Richard	J.	6983 South Friendship Road		Detroit	MI
1955-2452	Garcia	Michael	P.	46202 Broad Bend Avenue		Detroit	MI
2319-3068	Hastings	Francise	G.	6983 Sterling Parkway West	Apartment 16	Detroit	MI
3952-3948	Reynolds	Estelle	L.	25469 Weononah Street		Detroit	MI
5512-5239	Okano	Hayato	K.	1514 Wentworth Drive		Detroit	MI

Employees

ZIP	Phone	Birth	Sex	MStatus	Date Hired	Wage	Job Title
48203-1937	555-454-9043	76/04/22	M	M	97/06/13	$10.40	File Clerk
48201-4203	555-451-3304	66/08/12	M	M	91/10/13	$12.35	File Clerk
48203-4562	555-459-2345	83/03/01	F	S	99/11/08	$9.65	File Clerk
48201-2323	555-456-1383	73/05/06	F	S	97/12/05	$10.25	File Clerk
48202-1595	555-459-2493	75/02/24	M	M	00/04/15	$8.75	File Clerk

Employees

Department	Withholding
Records Management	3
Records Management	5
Records Management	3
Records Management	1
Records Management	3

OA15-3 (Goals 1 and 2)

The student is to work with two classmates on this project. The students are to contact two organizations or companies in your area and describe the types of records management systems that are used. They should include descriptions of the types of records maintained and storage mechanisms used. They should also describe any safety, security, or retention policies that are in place. Students can present their findings orally to the class. In addition, they should prepare a written report for you.

OA15-4 (Goals 1, 2, and 3)

The student is to write a short report (two or three pages) summarizing three articles on one of the current trends in records management listed at the end of the chapter. In addition, the student should submit a memorandum to you indicating how he or she feels this topic will impact records management policies or procedures within organizations.

KEY TO ONLINE RESEARCH APPLICATION

ORA15-5

Using the Internet, the student is to research one of the following topics:

microimage systems
document imaging
COLD systems

Students should choose two vendors with similar technology packages and compare and contrast their packages.

Students may consider the following questions when making their comparisons.

Are the prices similar or quite different?

What kinds of equipment are necessary to implement this system?

What kinds of user support and/or training does this organization provide?

What kinds of advantages do the vendors state will come from the implementation of this technology?

Students will present their findings orally to the class. In addition, they will prepare a written report. As part of the written report, students should indicate the impact this technology will have on records management.

KEY TO END OF PART 4 ACTIVITIES

Vocabulary Review: Part 4 (Chapters 14–15)

If you are grading these answers, each one is worth 2 points.

1. records management
2. records storage methods
3. numeric storage
4. terminal digit filing
5. chronologic storage system
6. indexing
7. coding
8. cross-referenced
9. requisition form
10. vital records
11. perpetual transfer
12. active records
13. suspension or hanging folders
14. important records
15. inspecting
16. database
17. decentralized storage
18. centralized storage
19. microfilm
20. microfiche
21. computer-output microfilm
22. computer-aided retrieval
23. computer output to laser disk
24. database management system
25. compact disk read-only memory

Language Skills Practice: Part 4 (Chapters 14–15)

If you are grading these answers, each one is worth 2 points.

1. We are reading several books in our English class; i.e., Toni Morrison's *Beloved,* Sandra Cisneros's *The House on Mango Street,* and Maya Angelou's *Wouldn't Take Nothing for My Journey Now.*
2. The CIA performs a vital function for our nation.
3. Reverend Jones was the minister who presided at the wedding.
4. The meeting will begin at 10:30 a.m.
5. Monday is a holiday.
6. Mary plans to take a course in management in the fall.
7. I am reading Tom Clancy's *Debt of Honor.*
8. We have a cottage on Lake Michigan.
9. The School of Medicine at the University of Michigan is considered one of the best in the nation.
10. The meeting was held at One Main Place.
11. Almost one hundred people were at the concert, and approximately fifty of those individuals were above 25.
12. The 2000s will bring even greater advances in technology than we have seen in the 1900s.
13. Although she looks much younger, she is almost eighty.
14. The twentieth century was filled with change.
15. Professors Leiberman and Kantz's book will be published this spring.
16. The scarf is hers.
17. The boat was named "The Lucky Lady."
18. Yes, I do plan to attend the graduation ceremony.
19. The individuals will be auditioning for the theatre production that will begin in May.
20. He is a world traveler.
21. The chair is not usable in my opinion.
22. I am so pleased that you were able to avoid an argument.
23. He bought potatoes, tomatoes, and onions at the market.
24. We have been picnicking all day.
25. My day has been unmanageable.

Part 5: Meetings, Travel, and Financial Documents

CHAPTER 16

MEETINGS AND CONFERENCES

According to research, the organizational time spent in meetings ranges from 50 percent for a top-level executive to 25 to 35 percent for middle-level managers. With the team approach that is now being used in many organizations, the office professional also may spend a number of hours each week in meetings. Since these hours are costly to the business or organization, it is important that meeting time be spent as productively as possible. This chapter will help the student develop the knowledge and skills to assist the executive in holding meetings that are productive for all members and, thus, an efficient use of organizational time.

STUDENT GOALS

1. Explain the elements of an effective meeting and utilize appropriate techniques in conducting meetings.
2. Identify and explain electronic meeting alternatives.
3. Define the responsibilities of the office professional for meetings and conferences.
4. Prepare minutes.

CHAPTER OUTLINE

  I. Introduction
 II. Your Goals
III. Meeting Effectiveness
      A. Unnecessary Meetings
      B. Necessary Meetings
      C. Role of Meeting Leader
         1. Make the Purpose and Objectives Clear
         2. Adhere to the Agenda
         3. Manage Time
         4. Encourage Participation
         5. Lead a Balanced and Controlled Discussion
         6. Handle Conflict
         7. Bring Closure to the Objectives
         8. Evaluate the Meeting
      D. Role of Meeting Participants
         1. Before the Meeting

         2. During the Meeting
         3. After the Meeting
 IV. Meeting Types
      A. Traditional Meetings
         1. Staff Meetings
         2. Committee Meetings
         3. Project Team Meetings
         4. Customer/Client Meetings
         5. Board of Directors Meetings
         6. Conventions and Conferences
      B. Electronic Meetings
         1. Audioconferencing
         2. Videoconferencing
         3. Data Conferencing
         4. Virtual Conferencing
         5. Advantages and Disadvantages of Electronic Meetings
      C. International Meetings
  V. The Executive's Role in Meetings
      A. Determine the Purpose
      B. Set the Objectives
      C. Determine Who Should Attend
      D. Determine the Number of Attendees
      E. Plan the Agenda
      F. Establish the Time and Place
 VI. The Office Professional's Role in Meetings
      A. Before the Meeting
         1. Discuss the Purpose, Objectives, and General Expectations with the Executive
         2. Gather Information
         3. Make Calendar Notations
         4. Reserve the Meeting Room
         5. Notify Participants
         6. Prepare the Agenda
         7. Prepare Materials for the Executive
         8. Prepare Materials for Attendees
         9. Order Equipment
        10. Determine the Seating Arrangement
        11. Order Food and Beverages
        12. Follow Up on the Meeting Notice

13. Check the Room Temperature
14. Prepare to Present
  B. During the Meeting
    1. Greet Guests
    2. Assist the Leader in Observing Parliamentary Procedure
    3. Take Notes and Minutes
    4. See that Food and Beverages Are Served
    5. Handle Special Problems
  C. After the Meeting
    1. Prepare the Notes or Minutes
    2. Perform Routine Follow-Up Duties
VII. Responsibilities of the Office Professional for Conferences and Conventions
  A. Before the Conference
    1. Arrange for Meeting Facilities
    2. Contact Outside Speakers
    3. Make Hotel and Travel Reservations
    4. Plan and Conduct Registration
    5. Assist with Planning and Arranging Meals and Receptions
    6. Prepare Evaluation Forms
  B. During the Conference
  C. After the Conference
VIII. Summary

IX. Key Terms
X. Professional Pointers
XI. Office Procedures Reinforcement
XII. Critical Thinking Activity
XIII. Office Applications
XIV. Online Research Application

TEACHING SUGGESTIONS

- Invite a hotel representative to explain the facilities and services they provide for conferences and conventions.
- Invite an officer from the local chapter of IAAP to discuss how their meetings are conducted.

KEY TO SUPPLEMENTAL EXERCISE

The student is given a supplemental exercise on page 109 of the Applications Workbook. The student is to prepare an agenda, using the information provided in the Applications Workbook. An agenda form is on the student template disk, file SE16. The student is not told when the Quality Leadership Board will be presented or by whom. The student is to pick up this omission and insert the information. Suggested information is given on the agenda shown here.

METROPOLITAN QUALITY COUNCIL

MEETING AGENDA
Wednesday, April 23,—

PLACE:	Wonderlin Hotel
	919 East Main Street
	Detroit, MI
TIME:	11:45 a.m.–1:40 p.m.
PARKING:	Wonderlin Garage
PURPOSE:	Implement Quality Control Measures
OBJECTIVES:	Propose a quality leadership board
	Outline the elements of an effective council
	Present a Latin-American Conference
	Introduce Board assessment

Time	Activity	Presenter	Action/Outcome
11:45	Lunch		
12:10–12:15	Introduction of Members/Guests	Jacqueline Ford	
12:15–12:35	Propose Quality Leadership Board	Jim Hamil	Approve officers
12:35–1:00	Outline How to be an Effective Council	Mike Clingenfelt	Build a team around common objectives
1:00–1:20	Present Latin-American Conference	Anita Leigh-Purcell	Organize committee
1:20–1:40	Introduce Assessment of Board	Bruce Waldrup	Receive ideas on benchmarking
1:40	Adjourn meeting	Jacqueline Ford	
1:50–3:00	Convene Executive Board Meeting	Jacqueline Ford	

KEY TO OFFICE PROCEDURES REINFORCEMENT

1. Describe the role of participants in a meeting.

   The meeting participants have responsibilities before, during, and after the meeting.

   Before the Meeting
   Participants are responsible for:
   - Responding to the meeting notice in a timely manner
   - Reading any materials sent out before the meeting
   - Evaluating the materials sent out in relation to the purpose of the meeting
   - Calling the executive to clarify any questions that they might have before the meeting

   During the Meeting
   Participants are responsible during the meeting for:
   - Being on time
   - Adhering to the agenda
   - Making contributions
   - Listening to other participants' contributions and responding
   - Respecting the leader's role
   - Not dominating the discussion
   - Being nonjudgmental of others' comments
   - Being courteous to each individual in the meeting
   - Taking notes, if necessary

   After the Meeting
   Once the meeting is over, the participants may be responsible for research, study, or action before the next meeting.

2. Describe the types of electronic meetings.

   Audioconferencing—Audioconferencing is a type of conference in which an unlimited number of participants use an audioconferencing unit to participate in a meeting. This unit may be as simple as a telephone with speakerphone capabilities, which provide hands-free communication and the amplifying and projecting of the speakers' voices. Or it may be a meeting that is set up through a conference operator or using software provided on the Internet.

   Videoconferencing—Videoconferencing is a system of transmitting audio and video between individuals at distant locations. Videoconferencing may be transmitted from a PC-based application (referred to as desktop videoconferencing) or by the use of a specially equipped room. Videoconferencing is interactive in that participants at all locations can see and respond to other participants.

   Data Conferencing—Data conferencing enables two or more people to communicate and collaborate as a group in real-time using the computer. Software is available to assist in data conferencing. The software allows participants to exchange information, send files, and chat with participants by keying text messages.

3. What is the executive's role in meetings?

   The executive's role in meetings is to:
   - Determine the purpose
   - Set the objectives
   - Determine who should attend
   - Determine the number of attendees
   - Plan the agenda
   - Establish the time and place

4. List the functions of the office professional in meetings.

   The office professional has responsibilities before, during, and after the meeting.

   Before the Meeting
   - Discuss the purpose, objectives, and general expectations with the executive
   - Gather information
   - Make calendar notations
   - Reserve the meeting room
   - Notify participants
   - Prepare the agenda
   - Prepare materials for attendees
   - Prepare materials for the executive
   - Order equipment
   - Determine the seating arrangement
   - Order food and beverages
   - Follow up on the meeting notice
   - Check the room temperature
   - Prepare to present (if needed)

   During the Meeting
   - Greet guests
   - Assist the leader in observing parliamentary procedure
   - Take notes and minutes
   - See that food and beverages are served
   - Handle special problems

   After the Meeting
   - Prepare the notes or minutes
   - Perform routine follow-up duties

5. List the responsibilities of the office professional in conferences and conventions.

   The office professional has responsibilities before, during, and after the conference.

   Before the Conference
   - Arrange for meeting facilities
   - Contact outside speakers
   - Make hotel and travel reservations
   - Plan and conduct registration
   - Assist with planning and arranging meals and receptions
   - Prepare evaluation forms

   During the Conference
   - Run errands
   - Help solve problems that occur

- Escort speakers to appropriate rooms
- Prepare and distribute an attendance list
- Collect evaluation forms
- Maintain expense records

After the Conference
- Perform general cleanup responsibilities
- Assist out-of-town guests and speakers with transportation to the airport
- Draft letters of appreciation
- Prepare expense reports
- Key the proceedings of the conference

KEY TO CRITICAL THINKING ACTIVITY

The student is given a case and asked to respond to the questions given here. Although answers will vary, here are suggested answers.

- What steps should Bess have taken in planning the meeting?

  Bess should have consulted an office procedures manual and carefully reviewed the responsibilities of the office professional in regard to meetings. She should have asked her employer about her expectations for the meeting. She should have set up two file folders (one for herself as she made arrangements for the meeting and one for her employer). In her file folder, Bess should have made a list of the items for which she was responsible. If Bess had any questions about making the arrangements, she should have asked her employer about his or her preferences.

- How might Bess have helped her employer in making a more professional appearance to the attendees?

  Bess should have talked with her employer when she was asked to set up the meeting. She should have explained that she had not arranged a meeting of this type and that she needed to know how her employer wanted it handled. Bess should have scheduled an appropriate conference room and informed her employer of its location; she also should have checked before the meeting to be certain that the conference room was available. Rather than going on a coffee break at the time of the meeting, she should have been in the room making sure that all arrangements were carried out. Also, she should have asked her employer if she wanted Bess to take notes at the meeting and if coffee or anything else should be served.

- Does Bess's employer have any responsibility for the poor meeting? If so, what are her responsibilities?

Yes, the employer does have some responsibility. When Bess first started to work, she should have had a session with her on what was expected. Then, when she asked Bess to set up the meeting, she again should have made her expectations clear. The employer should not assume that an employee knows how something is to be handled if the employer has not made the expectations clear.

- What should Bess's reactions to her employer's comments be?

  Bess should apologize for not understanding what should have been done. She should tell her employer that she wants to meet with her before the next meeting is scheduled to go over what should be done. In the meantime, Bess should research the office professional's responsibilities in planning meetings. She should let her employer know that she will do the research and that she will never make the same mistakes again.

KEY TO OFFICE APPLICATIONS

OA16-1 (Goals 1 and 3)

The student is to choose six to seven classmates to work with on this project. The task of the group is to conduct an effective meeting before their class members. They are to plan a meeting around one of the topics given below. They are to determine who will be the leader of the meeting. A meeting notice, an agenda, written materials (if there are any), and an evaluation form are to be prepared and given to the entire class before the meeting. Once the meeting has been held, the group and the other class members are to fill out the evaluation form. A copy of the meeting notice, agenda, written materials, and a compilation of the responses to the evaluation are to be submitted to you.

OA16-2 (Goal 4)

The student is to attend a professional meeting, for example, International Association of Administrative Professionals or a meeting of an organization on campus. The student is to take notes and then key the minutes in an acceptable format. A copy is to be submitted to you.

KEY TO ONLINE RESEARCH APPLICATION

ORA16-3 (Goal 2)

Using the Internet, the student is to search for current software and/or new developments in audio, video, and data conferencing. A brief report of the findings, with the sources noted, is to be submitted to you.

CHAPTER 17

TRAVEL ARRANGEMENTS

In this chapter, students are presented with the steps involved in making various travel arrangements. Methods of travel are discussed, but the emphasis is on airline travel. Both domestic and international travel arrangements are covered. The office professional's responsibility in trip preparation, while the employer is away, and upon the executive's return is presented.

STUDENT GOALS

1. Make travel arrangements.
2. Prepare itineraries.
3. Describe the duties to be performed while the executive is traveling and when he or she returns, and prepare an expense report.

CHAPTER OUTLINE

TEACHING SUGGESTIONS

• Ask a local travel agent to come to your class and discuss making appropriate travel arrangements. Travel agents can give further information on what things to consider when making arrangements.
• Bring a computer connected to the Internet to class to demonstrate using online flight schedules to make reservations or tentative plans. Demonstrate the variety of Internet sites devoted to travel (including hotel and rental car sites) that are available for the office professional.
• Bring a computer with specialized "trip-making" software to class. Demonstrate to the class how easy it is to use. If you

don't have access to this type of software, a variety of
Internet sites are available for your use.

KEY TO SUPPLEMENTAL EXERCISE

Using the Individual Trip Expense Report in OA17-3 as an
example, students are to create a spreadsheet that can be used
to record and calculate monthly travel expenses. Only totals
for each category should be recorded on the monthly report.
An example is shown below.

```
MONTHLY TRAVEL RESPONSE REPORT
TRAVELER'S NAME:  Juan Menendez
MONTH/YEAR:  January, 20
DATES OF TRAVEL      TRANSPORTATION    MEALS    LODGING    MISCELLANEOUS      TOTAL
Jan. 20-Jan. 23          783.96        59.35    177.35        26.05          1046.71
```

KEY TO OFFICE PROCEDURES REINFORCEMENT

1. Describe the advantages of joining an airline club.

    Membership in an airline club provides the business trav-
    eler with perks such as access to special airport lounges that
    are equipped with a variety of business equipment includ-
    ing computers, fax and copy machines, conference rooms,
    and telephones. Members also have access to current peri-
    odicals and newspapers. In addition, clubs may offer com-
    plimentary soft drinks, juice, coffee, pastries, and light
    snacks. Other clubs offer assistance with airline reserva-
    tions, seat selection, and boarding passes. Airline clubs are
    available for both the domestic and international business
    traveler.

2. Describe the responsibilities of the office professional if
    the executive is traveling by car.

    When an executive is traveling by car, the office profes-
    sional must determine whether or not the executive has a
    company-owned vehicle or the organization has a motor
    pool. The responsibilities for a car trip may include deter-
    mining the best route to follow, deciding where to stay for
    the night, and so on. Although a road map could be used, a
    variety of computer software programs are available to
    help plan a trip. In addition, some of these programs are
    available on the Internet. The office professional must
    make hotel reservations and provide directions to the hotel
    and meeting sites.

3. What kinds of information are necessary when making ho-
    tel reservations?

    When making hotel reservations, specify the room rate,
    choice of accommodations (king- or queen-size bed), num-
    ber of persons registering, date and approximate time of ar-
    rival, length of stay, and how the bill will be paid. If your
    employer is arriving after 6 p.m., you may need to guaran-

tee the room with a credit card number. Make sure to get the
confirmation number and give it to the employer.

4. Name and explain five considerations for international
    travel.

    Students should name and explain five of the following
    considerations for international travel:

    a) Be sensitive to the customs and cultures of other people.
        Learn appropriate greetings and farewells. Know lodg-
        ing and eating customs, such as tipping and proper dress
        for various functions.
    b) Plan for differences in time zones. Learn how to adjust
        to jet lag, and account for differences in time when mak-
        ing appointments.
    c) Expect to exchange business cards. Choose appropriate
        gifts for business associates.
    d) Check on luggage restrictions for weight and size for in-
        ternational travel.
    e) Determine if a passport or visa is required for entry and
        travel within a particular country.
    f) Determine the currency exchange rate and the places
        where the exchange rate may be more favorable than
        others.
    g) Learn what medical requirements must be met prior to
        traveling abroad. Be aware of health precautions for the
        country being visited.
    h) Make hotel reservations through a travel agent or
        through the airline you use.
    i) Determine the best and most cost-effective means of
        transportation once in the country.

5. What is an itinerary, and what should it include?

    An itinerary is a detailed outline of a trip. It should include
    flight numbers and departure and arrival times, hotel and
    motel reservations, appointments, car rental information,
    materials needed on the trip, and other helpful information.

KEY TO CRITICAL THINKING ACTIVITY

1. It is apparent that Brad does not know how to make the proper arrangements for a business trip. He should have asked Ms. Harris what she expected of him in preparing for the trip. Brad could have also asked other office support personnel what he should do in making these travel arrangements. Brad's first step should have been to establish a file when Ms. Harris told him about the trip to Orlando. He should have placed all notes about the trip in the folder; frequent reference to the folder would have reminded Brad about what Ms. Harris needed, such as the rental car. Brad should have admitted that he had failed to make the necessary arrangements. He should have keyed an itinerary that included all information about the trip; for example, flight information hotel reservations, car rentals, and appointments.

2. After Ms. Harris left on the trip, Brad should have used the time to sort the mail, refer any important correspondence to the person in charge, work on the files, keep a record of visitors and telephone calls, and read company periodicals. If he still had time, he could have offered to assist other office employees with projects they may have had.

3. Brad should learn from this situation that he must understand his employer's expectations. Brad should recognize those areas in which he has inadequate skills or knowledge, and he should make every attempt to correct them. He should learn to make ready use of an office reference manual to review standard office procedures. Brad must convey his willingness to overcome his deficiencies to his employer and then strive to meet her expectations.

KEY TO OFFICE APPLICATIONS

OA17-1 (Goal 1)

Divide the class into three groups (or allow students to form their own groups). Assign each group one of the countries that the team of executives will visit. The group should determine the steps necessary in preparing for the described business trip. Each group should prepare a written report (citing references) and prepare to share their research with the class in an oral presentation. Their research should include the following:

- The current exchange rate
- Visa/passport requirements
- Travel restrictions
- The suggestion for one gift to take
- Time zone differences
- Local airlines that serve the country
- Recommended ground transportation
- Current events that may have some significance or bearing on the trip.

OA17-2 (Goals 1 and 2)

Students are to create an itinerary from the information given in the textbook. A sample itinerary appears below.

OA17-3 (Goal 3)

Travel expenses for Mr. Menendez's trip to Chicago are to be calculated and recorded on the form provided in the students' Application Workbook on page 111. A hotel receipt with several of the expenses and a listing of additional expenses are

ITINERARY FOR JUAN MENENDEZ

January 21–23, 20-
Chicago, Illinois

(Day), January 21 (Richmond to Chicago)

7:35 a.m.	Leave Richmond Airport on US Air Flight 253 to Pittsburgh. Arrive Pittsburgh at 8:50 a.m.
9:35 a.m.	Leave Pittsburgh—Flight 307 to Chicago. Breakfast will be served.
10:15 a.m.	Arrive Chicago—O'Hare Airport. Budgett Car Rental, confirmation # 235292. Hotel reservation at Downtown's Central Plaza, confirmation # AR452038.
1:00 p.m.	Lunch with Kellouy Men Ho of Mendelson Machinery
3:00 p.m.	Business meeting with Ho from 3–5 p.m.

(Day), January 22 (Chicago)

9:00 a.m.	Meeting with Ken Martinez, Martinez Machinery
2:00 p.m.	Presentation to Board of Directors of Martinez Machinery
7:00 p.m.	Guest of Ken Martinez and Fred Yousef for dinner and the opera

(Day), January 23 (Chicago to Detroit)

8:00 a.m.	Breakfast meeting with Jeana Boziki of Rivers Corporation in hotel restaurant
10:20 a.m.	Leave Chicago, O'Hare Airport on US Air Flight 1708. Arrive in Detroit at 12:44 p.m.
3:30 p.m.	Appointment with Dr. Barnardski in your office

provided in the Applications Workbook on pages 112 and 113. Check to see that students deduct the $500 travel advance that Mr. Menendez received from the total amount due. A copy is provided on facing page.

KEY TO ONLINE RESEARCH APPLICATIONS

ORA17-4 (Goals 1 and 2)

Students are to choose a city in the United States to visit for one week. They are to follow specific instructions given in the textbook and prepare a report to be turned in to their instructor. This report should include a printed copy of the driving directions obtained from an Internet map service. In addition, the report should include the name of hotel accommodations as well as instructions to the hotel and a description of the services they provide (such as restaurants, weight room, conference facilities, pool, and so on). The report should also list one specialty restaurant the student will visit indicating the name of the restaurant, types of meals they offer, and price ranges. In addition, the report should include at least three local attractions they will visit. They should include the name of the attraction, a description of the attraction, hours of operation, and admission price.

ORA17-5 (Goal 1)

Students are to use the same destination as they used in ORA 17-4. They are to search the Internet and find at least two flights that will get them from their home city to the destination. Students will then prepare a memo to their instructor comparing the two options and indicating what option they would choose and why.

ORA17-6 (Goal 2)

Students are to use the information they obtained in ORA 17-4 and 17-5 to prepare an itinerary for their trip. They should include all times and activities for their weeklong trip.

ENTER ONLY ONE AMOUNT PER LINE, PER DAY.

People First International

INDIVIDUAL TRIP EXPENSE REPORT

NAME Juan Mendez

WEEK ENDING SATURDAY January 25

BAVE NO.　ENDING SPEEDOMETER　CHANGED DRIVER'S LICENSE NO.　TR. NO.

PERSONAL
MOTEL OR HOTEL Central Plaza Hotel
CITY Chicago
STATE Illinois

	SUNDAY	MONDAY	TUESDAY	WEDNESDAY	THURSDAY	FRIDAY	SATURDAY	TOTALS
11 ROOM CHARGE (ATTACH RECEIPT)			83 | 00	83 | 00		11 | 35		177 | 35
BREAKFAST				12 | 95	12 | 95	2 | 45		
LUNCH								
DINNER			25 | 75			5 | 25		
12 TOTAL MEALS			25 | 75	12 | 95	12 | 95	7 | 70		59 | 35
13 OTHER PERSONAL								
14 Transportation Airfare, Rail, Other			↓		645 | 00			645 | 00
15 Vehicle (Personal/Rental)					93 | 96			93 | 96
16 Other (Taxi, Parking)				30 | 00	15 | 00			45 | 00
17 MISCELLANEOUS ENTERTAINMENT (EXPLAIN)					(1) 12 | 95	(1) 5 | 10		18 | 05
18 Supplies/Business Related								
19 MISC. OTHER (EXPLAIN)					(2) 8 | 00			8 | 00
TOTAL FOR DAY								EXPENSES 1046 | 71
							LESS CASH ADVANCE	21 500 | 00
							ISSUE CHECK	22 546 | 71

EXPLAIN OF ENTERTAINMENT AND MISCELLANEOUS:
Mileage is calculated at 33.5 cents per mile

(1) Breakfast meeting with Juana Lopez, Riviera Corp.

(2) Valet Parking Tips

TRAVELER'S SIGNATURE Juan Mendez

CHAPTER 18

FINANCIAL DOCUMENTS

This chapter presents an overview of the office professional's responsibilities in providing financial assistance. Specific duties related to banking, accounting, payroll, investment, and insurance records will vary based on the scope of the office professional's job and the size of the business. In addition to the standard information on writing checks, reconciling a bank statement, and using special banking services, electronic banking is discussed. Analyzing financial statements is presented. Payroll deductions, such as social security and federal withholding tax, and investment information including stocks, bonds, and mutual funds are covered.

STUDENT GOALS

1. Describe electronic technology used in the banking industry.
2. Explain the basic financial statements and the various parts of the statements; prepare the following types of banking documents:

   • Checks
   • Deposit slips
   • Bank statement reconciliation

3. Explain payroll and other tax laws.
4. Define basic investment instruments and terminology.

CHAPTER OUTLINE

I. Introduction
II. Your Goals
III. Electronic Banking
   A. Automated Teller Machines (ATMs)
   B. Sophisticated Kiosks
   C. Debit Cards (Bank Cards)
   D. Smart Cards (Stored Value Cards)
   E. Direct Payroll Depositing
   F. Direct Withdrawals
   G. Computer Systems and Software Packages
   H. Loss of EFT Card
   I. The Future of Electronic Banking
IV. Banking Records and Procedures
   A. Checks
   B. Endorsements
   C. Deposits
   D. Bank Reconciliation
   E. Special Bank Services
     1. Certified Check
     2. Cashier's Check
     3. Bank Money Order
     4. Traveler's Check
     5. Safe-Deposit Box
V. Accounting Records
   A. Balance Sheet
   B. Income Statement
   C. Financial Statement Analysis
     1. Current Ratio
     2. Quick Ratio
   D. Petty Cash Fund
VI. Payroll Laws
   A. Fair Labor Standards Act
   B. Federal Insurance Contribution Act (Social Security)
   C. Federal, State, and Local Income Tax
   D. Unemployment Compensation Tax
   E. Other Deductions
   F. Other Taxes
     1. Property Tax
     2. Sales Tax
     3. License Taxes
VII. Investments
   A. Stocks
     1. Kinds of Stocks
     2. Stock Exchanges
     3. The NASD
     4. The Internet
     5. Stock Quotations
   B. Mutual Funds
   C. Bonds
   D. IRAs
VIII. Summary
IX. Key Terms
X. Professional Pointers
XI. Office Procedures Reinforcement
XII. Critical Thinking Activity
XIII. Office Applications
XIV. Online Research Applications

TEACHING SUGGESTIONS

- Ask all members of the class to discuss the types of electronic banking equipment they have had experiences with and have them describe their experiences to the class.
- Ask someone from your local bank or credit union to discuss the banking industry (including advances in electronic banking) with your class.
- Ask someone from a local accounting firm to discuss accounting records with your class.
- Break the students into groups and divide the chapter into sections. Have each group present information from their assigned text section to the remainder of the students in the course.

KEY TO SUPPLEMENTAL EXERCISE

The student is given a supplemental exercise on page 125 of the Applications Workbook. Students are asked to obtain current stock quotes of the day by logging into the Microsoft Network home page http://www.msn.com, by logging into any other Web site of their choice, or by gathering information from the local newspaper. They are to create a table that shows the last quote, the change, and the percentage changed. Students should print a copy of their tables.

KEY TO OFFICE PROCEDURES REINFORCEMENT

1. Name and describe the two types of debit cards.

   The two types of debit cards are online and offline. Online debit cards require the use of a PIN to initiate the transaction. With this system, online debit transactions are sent through ATM networks and subtract funds from accounts immediately. Offline debit cards are very similar to credit cards; in fact, the transactions flow over the credit card network. With offline debit cards, the transactions are not immediate; they usually require a few days to settle or for the payment to transfer. A local area network links various types of equipment used within a building or several buildings within the same geographic area. It consists of transmission cable to transmit the information, plus interface units to link the various pieces of equipment to the cable.

2. List the advantages to employee and employer of direct payroll deposit.

   Some of the advantages of direct payroll depositing to the employer are:

   - Eliminates the time and expense of writing paychecks
   - Lower security measures needed in processing and distributing vouchers as opposed to checks.
   - Reduces postage by not mailing checks.
   - Decreases the possible loss or theft of paychecks.

Advantages to the employee include:

- Convenience—does not have to drive to the bank or wait in line to make a deposit
- Provides for the payroll check to be deposited in the bank even when the employee is on vacation or on a business trip

3. Name and explain the difference in the three types of check endorsements.

   - A blank endorsement requires only the signature of the payee.
   - An endorsement in full transfers ownership to another person or business, but the name of the person to whom the check is to be transferred is written before the endorser's signature.
   - A restrictive endorsement transfers ownership for a specific purpose.

4. List and describe the types of special checks that are offered by banks.

   - A certified check is a business or personal check that is guaranteed by the bank on which it is drawn. In order to certify a check, a bank official investigates the drawer's account to see if there are sufficient funds to cover the check. The drawer's account is immediately charged with the amount of the check. A small fee is usually charged to certify a check.
   - A cashier's check is issued by a bank and drawn on the bank's own funds. A cashier's check can be purchased by giving the bank cash or a check for the amount of money desired. A small fee is required by the bank for writing the check.
   - A bank money order is sold by the bank and states that a certain amount of money is to be paid to the person named on the money order. Normally cashable at any bank in the United States or abroad, the money order is negotiable and can be transferred by endorsement.
   - The traveler's check facilitates paying for expenses when traveling. Traveler's checks are sold in various denominations by banks, travel agencies, or American Express. A small fee may be charged, depending on the amount purchased. When traveler's checks are purchased, each check must be signed by the purchaser.

5. Explain what a current ratio of 2.5 to 1 would indicate about the financial position of a company.

   The current ratio is determined by dividing assets by liabilities. The ratio indicates the debt-paying ability of a company. A current ratio of 2.5 to 1 means that a company receives $2.50 for every dollar that is spent.

KEY TO CRITICAL THINKING ACTIVITY

1. Sandi has made several mistakes in managing the petty cash fund. She should not have borrowed money from the

fund. Sandi should not have used any money for which she did not place a receipt in the box or make a record of the transaction. She should never leave the petty cash box unlocked or in plain view.

2. A register, much like a checkbook register, could be used to record deductions from the account. Information such as the person to whom the money was given, date, and purpose of the transaction should be recorded. The petty cash box should be locked at all times.

3. Sandi should try to make a list of the transactions she made from the petty cash fund. After balancing the account as closely as she can, she should then discuss the situation with the president. Sandi should admit that she was not responsible enough with the fund, and she should outline the measures she plans to take to prevent these kinds of problems in the future.

KEY TO OFFICE APPLICATIONS

OA18-1 (Goal 1)

Working in groups of three, the students are to write a short report (two or three pages) summarizing three articles on electronic banking. In addition, the students should be prepared to present their findings orally to the class.

OA18-2 (Goal 2)

Several banking transactions are required in this job. Students are to create two banking deposits and write five checks based on information provided. The forms for these transactions are in the Applications Workbook. Completed forms appear on pages 94 and 95.

OA18-3 (Goal 2)

This job requires students to reconcile a bank statement for the Rotary club. A bank reconcilement form is provided in their Applications Workbook, which they should use in verifying the bank statement. A sample reconciliation is shown on page 96.

Students are to also compose a letter to report a $25 error made by the bank on behalf of the Rotary Club. They should follow the instructions on the bank's reconcilement form to report this error. A sample letter is provided on page 97.

OA18-4 (Goal 3)

This job requires students to prepare a weekly payroll. The payroll has previously been prepared manually; students are to create a spreadsheet that will aid in calculating the payroll more efficiently each week for the ten hourly employees. Data on the employees needed to calculate the payroll is provided in the Applications Workbook on page 123. Students must determine earnings from regular and overtime pay, calculate FICA tax and withholding tax based on rates provided, and deduct hospitalization that is provided in the Applications Workbook. The total net earnings are calculated for the weekly payroll. A sample payroll is provided below.

WEEKLY PAYROLL

People First International

Employee Name	Regular Hours	Hourly Rate	Hourly Earnings	Overtime Hours	Overtime Earnings	Total Earnings	FICA 7.65%	Withholding Percent	Withholding Amount	Hosp	Net Earnings
Boone, Robert	40	9.75	$390.00	0	$0.00	$390.00	$29.84	9%	$35.10	$30.00	$295.07
Keith, Shawn	40	11.25	$450.00	0	$0.00	$450.00	$34.43	10%	$45.00	$35.00	$335.58
Kay, Anita	40	8.75	$350.00	8	$105.00	$455.00	$34.81	9%	$40.95	$30.00	$349.24
Lane, Jose	40	9.75	$390.00	2	$29.25	$419.25	$32.07	9%	$37.73	$30.00	$319.44
Lin, Mo	40	9.25	$370.00	5	$69.38	$439.38	$33.61	8%	$35.15	$30.00	$340.61
Mark, Isabelle	40	8.25	$330.00	0	$0.00	$330.00	$25.25	8%	$26.40	$30.00	$248.36
North, Walter A.	40	9.75	$390.00	4	$58.50	$448.50	$34.31	9%	$40.37	$35.00	$338.82
Park, Quincy E	40	8.2	$328.00	0	$0.00	$328.00	$25.09	8%	$26.24	$30.00	$246.67
Ramos, Amelia	40	9.75	$390.00	0	$0.00	$390.00	$29.84	9%	$35.10	$40.00	$285.07
Stein, Lisa	40	11.25	$450.00	0	$0.00	$450.00	$34.43	10%	$45.00	$35.00	$335.58

NO. 1001 $ _45.83_

DATE _July 10_ 20 _--_

TO _Time Square Florist_

FOR _2 arrangements/ delivered_

	DOLLARS	CENTS
BAL BRG'T FOR'D	2300	00
AMT. DEPOSITED	400	00
TOTAL	2700	00
AMT. THIS CHECK	45	83
BAL. CAR'D FOR'D	2654	17

July 10 20 _--_

PAY TO THE ORDER OF _Time Square Florist_ $45.83

Forty-Five and 83/100 ———————— DOLLARS

ATLEE ROTARY CLUB

Essex Bank

Detroit, MI 48209-1622

⑆ 1110099 2⑆ 130 ‖ 66687 ‖

NO. 1002 $ _42.26_

DATE _July 10_ 20 _--_

TO _Fast Print_

FOR _printing: membership directory - speakers bureau_

	DOLLARS	CENTS
BAL BRG'T FOR'D	2654	17
AMT. DEPOSITED	0	
TOTAL	2654	17
AMT. THIS CHECK	42	26
BAL. CAR'D FOR'D	2611	91

July 10 20 _--_

PAY TO THE ORDER OF _Fast Print_ $42.26

Forty-two and 26/100 ——————— DOLLARS

ATLEE ROTARY CLUB

Essex Bank

Detroit, MI 48209-1622

⑆ 1110099 2⑆ 130 ‖ 66687 ‖

NO. 1003 $ _167.00_

DATE _July 10_ 20 _--_

TO _Atlee Hardware_

FOR _Flag Pole & Flag_

	DOLLARS	CENTS
BAL BRG'T FOR'D	2611	91
AMT. DEPOSITED	0	0
TOTAL	2611	91
AMT. THIS CHECK	167	00
BAL. CAR'D FOR'D	2444	91

July 10 20 _--_

PAY TO THE ORDER OF _Atlee Hardware_ $167.00

One Hundred Sixty Seven and no/100 ——— DOLLARS

ATLEE ROTARY CLUB

Essex Bank

Detroit, MI 48209-1622

⑆ 1110099 2⑆ 130 ‖ 66687 ‖

NO. 1004 $ _375.00_

DATE _July 10_ 20 _--_

TO _Lipscomb Appliance_

FOR _Air conditioner & TV/VCR comb. unit_

	DOLLARS	CENTS
BAL BRG'T FOR'D	2444	91
AMT. DEPOSITED	0	0
TOTAL	2444	91
AMT. THIS CHECK	375	00
BAL. CAR'D FOR'D	2069	91

July 10 20 _--_

PAY TO THE ORDER OF _Lipscomb Appliance_ $375.00

Three Hundred Seventy Five and no/100 —— DOLLARS

ATLEE ROTARY CLUB

Essex Bank

Detroit, MI 48209-1622

⑆ 1110099 2⑆ 130 ‖ 66687 ‖

OA18-2 (CONTINUED)

Checking Account Deposit Ticket

ATLEE ROTARY CLUB

DATE ___ July 7 ___ 20 _ _

CASH	CURRENCY		
	COIN		
C H E C K S		100	00
		100	00
		100	00
		100	00
TOTAL		400	00
LESS CASH RECEIVED		-	-
NET DEPOSIT		400	00

BE SURE EACH ITEM IS
PROPERLY ENDORSED

Essex Bank   Detroit MI 48209-1622

⑆⑈00999 2⑈   ⑈30⑈⑆6668 7⑈⑈

CHECKS AND OTHER ITEMS ARE RECEIVED FOR DEPOSIT SUBJECT TO THE TERMS AND CONDITIONS OF THIS BANK'S COLLECTION AGREEMENT.

Checking Account Deposit Ticket

ATLEE ROTARY CLUB

DATE ___ July 31 ___ 20 _ _

CASH	CURRENCY		
	COIN		
C H E C K S		100	00
		100	00
TOTAL		200	00
LESS CASH RECEIVED		-	-
NET DEPOSIT		200	00

BE SURE EACH ITEM IS
PROPERLY ENDORSED

Essex Bank   Detroit MI 48209-1622

⑆⑈00999 2⑈   ⑈30⑈⑆6668 7⑈⑈

CHECKS AND OTHER ITEMS ARE RECEIVED FOR DEPOSIT SUBJECT TO THE TERMS AND CONDITIONS OF THIS BANK'S COLLECTION AGREEMENT.

OA18-2 (CONTINUED)

NO. 1005 $ 414.⁰⁰

DATE July 31   20 _ _   No. 1005

TO Becky Coviello

FOR Recycling Bins &
Supplies

	DOLLARS	CENTS
BAL. BRGT FORD	2069	91
AMT. DEPOSITED	200	00
TOTAL	2269	91
AMT. THIS CHECK	414	00
BAL. CARD FORD	1855	91

July 31   20 _ _   No. 1005

$ 414.⁰⁰

PAY TO THE
ORDER OF   Becky Coviello

Four Hundred Fourteen   and no/100 ___ DOLLARS

ATLEE ROTARY CLUB

Essex Bank   Detroit MI 48209-1622

⑆⑈00999 2⑈   ⑈30⑈⑆6668 7⑈⑈

CHANGE OF ADDRESS NOTICE .

Name _____ Account # _____

New address _____

_____ Zip _____

If you move, please notify us
immediately in writing.
Detach and return this form.

Member's Signature _____ Date _____

Home Phone (   ) _____ Work Phone (   ) _____

Social Security # _____

☐ Check here if you have a Bank VISA, VISA Gold, or MasterCard.

- -

CHECKING ACCOUNT RECONCILEMENT
Use this form to balance your
checking account.

List checks outstanding (checks written but
not shown on this statement).

CHECK NO.	AMOUNT
1003	167 00
1005	414 00
TOTAL OUTSTANDING CHECKS	581 00

IN CASE OF ERRORS OR QUESTIONS ABOUT YOUR STATEMENT

If you think your statement is wrong, or if you need more information about a
transaction on your statement, write us as soon as possible on a separate sheet
at the address shown on your statement. **We must hear from you no later than
60 days after we sent you the first statement on which the error or problem
appeared.** You can telephone us, but doing so will not preserve your rights.

In your letter give us the following information:
1. Your name and account number.
2. The dollar amount of the suspected error.
3. Describe the error and explain, if you can, why you believe there is an
    error. If you need more information, describe the item you are unsure
    about.

IN CASE OF ERRORS OR QUESTIONS ABOUT YOUR ELECTRONIC TRANSFERS
TELEPHONE US AT 804-328 -0000/TOLL FREE 1 800 555-0099 OR WRITE US
AT P.O. BOX 651, RICHMOND, VA 23225-5223, as soon as you can if you think
your statement or receipt is wrong or if you need more information about a transfer listed on the statement or receipt. **We must hear from you no later than 60
days after we sent your FIRST statement on which the problem or error
appeared.**

1. Tell us your name and account number.
2. Describe the error or the transfer you are unsure about, and explain as
    clearly as you can why you believe it is an error or why you need more
    information.
3. Tell us the dollar amount of the suspected error.

We will investigate your complaint and will correct any error promptly. If we take
more than 10 business days to do this, we will recredit your account for the
amount you think is in error, so that you will have use of the money during the
time it takes to complete our investigation.

IMPORTANT INFORMATION
Information on this statement is being reported to the Internal Revenue Service.

STATEMENT BALANCE	2122.74
ADD DEPOSIT MADE BUT NOT SHOWN ON THIS STATEMENT	+ 200.00
SUBTOTAL	2322.74
SUBTRACT TOTAL OUTSTANDING CHECKS	− 581.00
TOTAL	1741.74

Remember to subtract from your
check register any fees or charges
for printed checks.

This should be the balance in
your check register.

(current date)

Essex Bank
P. O. Box 651
Detroit, MI 48209-1622

Ladies and Gentlemen:

On behalf of the Atlee Rotary Club, I am reporting an error that was made in June.
Our account number is 130-66687. Apparently a $25 service fee was charged against
our account.

Your bank was chosen for the club's account because you do not charge a fee for
minimum balances for non-profit organizations. In June our account did fall below
$1,000, and the fee was erroneously charged to us.

Please credit the account with the $25.

Sincerely,

Rue Washburn, Treasurer
Atlee Rotary Club

xx

KEY TO ONLINE RESEARCH APPLICATIONS

ORA 18-5 (Goal 3)

Student answers will vary depending on the current social security percentage and base salary amounts. Students need to look up the correct numbers and calculate the amount of tax. (The percent of 7.65 and base salary of $72,600 is used to illustrate correct answers for the first and last salary in the table.)

Employee Number	Yearly Salary	Amount of Social Security Tax
15–250	$37,550	$2,872.96 (37,555*7.65%)
16–438	132,000	$6,415.20 (72,600*7.65%) + (59,400*1.45%)

ORA 18-6 (Goal 4)

Using the Internet, the students are to research traditional and Roth IRAs. They are to discuss similarities and differences in the types of IRA accounts available and the restrictions for each of the accounts. Students should submit this information to you in the form of a report.

KEY TO END OF PART 5 ACTIVITIES

Vocabulary Review: Part 5 (Chapters 16–18)

If you are grading these answers, each one is worth 2 points.

1. teleconferencing
2. videoconferencing
3. data conferencing
4. synergy
5. agenda
6. rectangular arrangement
7. jet lag
8. passport
9. visa
10. itinerary
11. NT-ATM
12. drawer
13. payee
14. endorsement
15. restrictive endorsement
16. certified check
17. balance sheet or statement of financial position
18. income statement
19. stock
20. bond
21. mutual fund company
22. assets
23. liabilities
24. cashier's check
25. check truncation, check retention, or check safekeeping

Language Skills Practice: Part 5 (Chapters 16–18)

If you are grading these answers, each one is worth 2 points, including the rule on the word division questions.

1. The address of the company is 1125 East Grand Avenue.
2. The quarterback has No. 18 on his jersey.
3. He lives on the north side of Highway 31.
4. Please refer to page 2 in the book.
5. Reba Blackshire is the new president-elect of the organization.
6. I wrote Aunt Patricia and Uncle Norris last evening.
7. We hung new venetian blinds in our home.
8. The candy bar costs 75 cents.
9. The train runs this route at 9 p.m. and 12 midnight.
10. The folder should have one-half cut tabs.
11. We will be going to the movie in a while.
12. The meeting will be held at noon.
13. He graciously accepted the gift.
14. The company is two miles farther.
15. The post is stationary.
16. Whom shall I ask to do the presentation?
17. My conscience told me that the action was wrong.
18. He dropped the ball.
19. The psychologist pointed out that we have differing gifts.
20. apple
    Rule: Do not divide words of five or fewer letters.
21. careless-ness
    Rule: When a base word ends in a double consonant, divide between the base word and the suffix.
22. self-control
    Rule: Divide hyphenated compound words at existing hyphens only.

Part 6: The Office Professional's Career

CHAPTER 19

EMPLOYMENT AND ADVANCEMENT

Throughout this course, the students have been focusing on developing the knowledge and skills that will help them be successful as office professionals. However, before they can put these skills to good use on the job, they must be successful in getting the job. This chapters focuses on developing these skills. Job application skills (including writing a letter of application, preparing a resume, and developing interviewing skills) are presented. In addition, job advancement skills are discussed.

STUDENT GOALS

1. Write a letter of application.
2. Prepare a resume.
3. Complete an employment application.
4. Develop and use interview skills.
5. Review and revise your career plan.

CHAPTER OUTLINE

XII.   Critical Thinking Activity
XIII. Office Applications
XIV. Online Research Application

TEACHING SUGGESTIONS

• Invite a human resources director to talk with the class about interview "do's" and "don'ts."
• Invite an office professional to talk about job advancement.
• Invite a supervisor to discuss employee performance appraisals.

KEY TO SUPPLEMENTAL EXERCISE

The student is given a supplemental exercise on page 136 of the Applications Workbook. He or she is asked to do the following:

• Interview an individual who has recently changed jobs. Learn why the change was made and what steps were taken regarding the change in employment. Ask the interviewee what he or she learned from the experience.
• Interview a supervisor; ask the person the following:
  — In your experience, what contributes to employees losing their jobs?
  — What can employees do to enhance their growth potential?

The student is to prepare a written report, listing the names and company affiliations of the interviewees; the report is to be submitted to you.

KEY TO OFFICE PROCEDURES REINFORCEMENT

1. List the elements of an effective letter of application.
   An effective letter of application includes these elements:
   —An introductory paragraph that generates interest in the application and the purpose for writing the letter
   —A second paragraph that highlights the applicant's key strengths and abilities
   —A summary statement that briefly gives the applicant's education and experience
   —A statement that compels action on the part of the company
   —A statement of appreciation
2. List and explain the standard parts of a resume.
   —Heading
   —Objective
   —Relevant skills
   Employment history
   Education
   Professional accomplishments
   Reference section
3. List ten helpful hints for making a good impression during an interview.

The student may list any ten of the following:
—Dress appropriately.
—Keep the amount of jewelry to a minimum.
—Be well groomed.
—Get a good night's rest before the interview.
—Carry a briefcase.
—Stand and walk with head erect and shoulders back.
—Greet the receptionist with a friendly smile.
—Say "thank you" often.
—Give a firm handshake.
—Wait to sit until invited to do so.
—Do not play with hair or jewelry.
—Don't invade the personal space of others.
—Don't furrow your brow or tense your jaw.
—Don't nod your head excessively.
—Maintain appropriate eye contact.
—Display good humor and a ready smile.
—Be discreet.
—Show genuine interest in what the interviewer says.
—Don't talk too much.
—Try to understand your prospective employer's needs.
—Do not smoke or chew gum.
—Answer questions completely and succinctly.
—At the close of the interview, attempt to determine what the next steps will be.
4. How should you conduct yourself during a performance appraisal?
   —Accept the evaluation as a chance for you to learn and grow.
   —Listen openly to what the evaluator is saying.
   —Offer any significant information relating to your performance that the evaluator may not know.
   —Maintain eye contact with the evaluator.
   —Discuss issues honestly; maintain a calm and professional demeanor.
   —Ask the evaluator to provide specific examples of general statements.
   —Accept an adverse evaluation as a criticism of your performance—not of you as an individual.
   —Resolve to correct your mistakes.
   —Accept the evaluation as the organization's way of emphasizing your performance strengths, pointing out any performance weaknesses, and helping you improve your performance.
5. Explain how you should handle an exit interview.
   —Do not make any derogatory remarks about your supervisor or the company.
   —State your reasons for leaving clearly and concisely.
   —Do not burn any bridges.

KEY TO CRITICAL THINKING ACTIVITY

The student is given a case and asked to answer the two questions given here. Although answers will vary, suggested responses are given.

- What advice do you have for Emily? What did she do wrong in the interviews?

  Emily is entirely too self-effacing, shows little confidence in her ability, and tends to downplay or not even mention her accomplishments. By personality type, she is shy and introverted. However, Emily was an excellent student and has done well in her temporary work. She should begin to believe in her abilities. It may be good for Emily to talk with a trusted friend, advisor, or family member about her strengths. Here are suggestions that could be made to Emily for improvement.

- Believe in yourself. Sit down and list all of your strengths; take pride in them. Practice talking about these strengths to a good friend or advisor.
- Let the interviewer know that you were an excellent student.
- Explain that you have been working for a temporary agency the last year because you wanted to determine where your skills would fit. State (in a very positive tone) that now you know you want to work in the technical field. Talk about what you learned as a temporary employee, working for seven different firms. Let the interviewer know that you were offered full-time jobs but turned them down because you had not decided where you wanted to work.
- Don't make the good grades sound negative by immediately adding that you did not do anything outside of school work. Stress your good grades. If asked about extracurricular activities, you might say: "I didn't become involved because I had very limited extra time."
- Highlight your strengths; make a list before the interview; go over the list carefully. Make certain that you are prepared to talk about them proudly. Don't brag, but do be self-assured. You can also say something such as, "I enjoy learning, and I always look forward to learning new things." Make the need to continue to learn a positive rather than a negative.
- Think through the questions you want to ask the interviewer before the interview. Be prepared to ask thoughtful questions.
- Practice making eye contact with people before the interview. Only look down temporarily to break the sense of staring.

KEY TO OFFICE APPLICATIONS

OA19-1 (Goals 1, 2, and 3)

The student is asked to do the following:

- Using the newspaper or Internet as sources, find a position in which he or she is interested in applying.
- Complete an employment application (given in the workbook).
- Prepare a letter of application.
- Prepare a resume.

Copies of all documents are to be submitted to you, along with a copy of the job notice or the source of the notice. All documents will vary. In grading, be certain that the student is responding to the techniques given in this chapter.

OA19-2 (Goal 4)

The student is asked to select three classmates to work with on this project. The students are to alternate between being the interviewer, the interviewee, and the evaluator. They are to answer the questions given below and fill out evaluation forms. The interviewee is to fill out a self-evaluation form and the evaluators are to fill out appraisal forms. The entire group is to discuss how improvement can be achieved once each student has answered the questions.

- What are your goals?
- What are your strengths?
- What are your weaknesses?
- What do you know about the company?
- Why do you think you are qualified for this position?
- Why did you leave your previous job?
- Do you have any questions?

The student is given some help in answering the questions in the Applications Workbook, pp. 135–136. The student is not asked to submit anything to you on this job.

OA19-3 (Goal 5)

Using the self-evaluation chart completed in Chapter 1 and the stress audit completed in Chapter 3, the student is to reevaluate himself or herself. These reevaluations are not to be submitted to you.

Using the career plan that was prepared in Chapter 1, the student is to review, analyze, and revise the plan to reflect current career goals. Also the student is asked to write a mission statement. Both the revised career plan and the mission statement are to be submitted to you.

KEY TO ONLINE RESEARCH APPLICATION

ORA 19-4 (Goal 4)

The student is to search the Web for job openings in his or her area of interest and to find out all he or she can about one company that has job openings. The findings are to be reported to the class.

CHAPTER 20

LEADERSHIP AND MANAGEMENT

As the office professional gains experience, she or he may have the opportunity to supervise one or more employees. Being an effective supervisor demands an understanding and application of effective leadership and management principles. In this chapter, the student is introduced to these principles.

STUDENT GOALS

1. Define leadership
2. Identify the major tasks of leadership.
3. Identity and improve leadership skills.

CHAPTER OUTLINE

TEACHING SUGGESTIONS

- Ask your students to collect and bring to class for discussion three recent newspaper, television, Internet, or periodical (*Fortune* is a good source) articles on international leadership. Use the session as a time to talk about the importance of ethical leadership internationally.
- Invite a human resources director to discuss: (1) laws and regulations that apply to interviewing and (2) effective evaluation systems.

KEY TO SUPPLEMENTAL EXERCISE

A case is presented on page 139 of the Applications Workbook. Students are to work in groups of four to six people to discuss the case and offer suggestions to improve the situation. Here are suggested responses to the items.

1. Is there a problem with the supervisor? If so, what is it and how should it be handled?

   Yes, there is a problem. The supervisor has a very negative view of people. The supervisor believes that all people are lazy and dislike work, that individuals must be controlled and disciplined, and that the average person has little ambition.

   If so, how should it be handled? The supervisor's attitude toward people must be dealt with by upper management. The division manager, to whom the supervisor reports, must talk with the supervisor about how he manages. The division manager should ask the supervisor to develop a plan of action for improvement. The supervisor probably will not be able to change his attitude and philosophy without some help. The supervisor should be asked to attend workshops, take a course, read, and so forth on the differences between leadership and management. The supervisor should be asked to apply techniques he learns in dealing with the people he supervises.

2. What are the problems in the workgroup? How should they be handled?

The problems in the workgroup include personal problems, absenteeism, dissension in the workgroup, low production rates, and failure to observe working hours. The division manager should ask the supervisor to develop a plan of action immediately to solve each of these problems. The division manager should review and approve the plan (or make additional suggestions). The division manager should then talk with the supervisor approximately every two weeks about whether or not improvements are occurring.

Since his underlying philosophy of management is a negative one, the supervisor is going to have to want to change and grow. This will probably be difficult. If the supervisor cannot make the necessary changes (after being given a significant amount of time—possibly six months), the division manager needs to make a tough decision. Should the supervisor be reassigned to another job in another part of the organization, assuming he has the skills to do the job? Should he be fired? These types of decisions are very difficult. However, the division manager cannot let one person impact the performance of an entire unit. The assumption is made here that the workgroup can improve its performance radically since it was functioning very well before the new supervisor began.

This case is a good one to talk with the class about the differences between leadership and management and how philosophy and values affect the way we view situations.

KEY TO OFFICE PROCEDURES REINFORCEMENT

1. Explain the difference between leadership and management.

Leadership and management are part of the same continuum, with leadership encompassing all aspects of management and management being an integral part of effective leadership. Leadership is the process of persuading others to take action that is consistent with the purpose of the leader or the group's shared purpose. Management in its traditional sense is defined as the performance of the tasks or activities that are necessary in managing an organization—planning, organizing, leading, and controlling. Management deals with a bottom-line focus—how can certain tasks be performed efficiently? Leadership deals with the overall picture—what should be accomplished in the organization? Managers are people who do things right and leaders are people who do the right thing.

2. List and explain five characteristics of the effective leader.

- Builds a shared vision—The leader not only has a vision in his or her head and heart but is able to help others see the same vision. The leader is able to coalesce individuals around a vision and help them live the vision through the performance of activities that make the vision a reality.
- Lives by a set of values—Leaders must not only stand firmly on moral principles, but they must work within the organization to define what moral principles the organization will live by and see that these principles are carried out in the daily life of an organization.
- Uses power appropriately—Power must be distributed throughout the organization. The effective leader empowers others by providing employees access to information, allowing them to take on more responsibility, and encouraging employees to have a voice in decision making.
- Engenders trust—Effective leaders create a climate of trust throughout the organization by consistently living by a stated set of values, being reliable and predictable, and being unshakably fair in public and private.
- Rewards risk taking—The organization cannot take refuge in status quo, conformity to the norm, or security in the past. The effective leader understands this stance, takes educated risks, and helps employees take risks.

3. Identify seven leadership tasks.

- Envisioning goals
- Affirming values
- Managing
- Motivating
- Achieving unity
- Explaining and teaching
- Renewing

4. Explain the difference between long-range planning and tactical planning.

Long-range planning is the process by which the ideas from strategic thinking are translated into an action format. Long-range planning helps the ideas turn into reality. It identifies directions that must be carried out, generally, in a three- to five-year time frame. Tactical planning is the process of making detailed decisions about what the organization intends to accomplish, how and when it will be accomplished, who will be accountable, the resources required, and how the accomplishment will be evaluated. Tactical planning is generally done for a period of one year.

5. List and explain five effective evaluation guidelines.

The student may list and explain any five of the following:

- Evaluate performance on a day-to-day basis.
- Know yourself. Know who you are, what your needs are, and what your values are.
- Allow adequate time for evaluation.
- Give credit where credit is due.

- Be fair.
- Listen to what the person is saying.
- Avoid personal areas.
- Establish attainable objectives.

KEY TO CRITICAL THINKING ACTIVITY

The student is given a case and asked to respond to these questions. Answers will vary; here are suggested responses.

1. Did upper management make a mistake in promoting Mr. Saga? If so, what should they have considered before promoting Mr. Saga?

   It is not clear whether a mistake has been made since upper management has not addressed the issue and attempted to help Mr. Saga improve. However, they may have made a mistake—time will tell. The assumption is made from what happened that upper management considered only the recommendation of the department manager and Mr. Saga's performance in his previous job. Upper management should have given consideration to whether or not Mr. Saga showed any signs of leadership ability.

2. Should the employees tell Mr. Saga how they are feeling? If so, what should they say?

   Yes, they should attempt to talk with him. They should approach him in an open manner and tell him that they are concerned that they do not have more voice in what is happening in the department. They should offer suggestions about improvements; they should go into the meeting having carefully thought through suggestions—not merely presenting a problem. They should tell Mr. Saga that they would like the chance to meet with him as a group every week or every week other week to discuss department directions.

3. What suggestions would you make to Mr. Saga so that he might become a more effective manager?

   - Get out of his office.
   - Listen to what his workgroup is saying; be observant of what they are thinking from what is not said and the nonverbal behavior of the group.
   - Involve employees in setting new policies and procedures; or, if it is not possible to involve them due to policies being set at a higher level, advise them immediately when new policies and/or procedures are set.
   - Meet with the workgroup every week or two to go over department directions.
   - Make it a point to talk individually with each member of the department every week.
   - Read and/or attend seminars and classes on effective leadership.

KEY TO OFFICE APPLICATIONS

OA20-1 (Goals 1 and 2)

The student is to select three classmates to work with on this project. They are to interview two supervisors and ask them the questions given below. Their findings are to be recorded in a short report, giving the names and organizations of the people interviewed. The written report is to be submitted to you and an oral report given to the class.

- How would you define leadership?
- How did you develop your leadership skills?
- What characteristics does a leader possess?
- Does your organization have a published mission and value statement? If so, how was it developed? (Ask for a copy of the statement.)
- How is the planning process conducted in your organization?
- What process do you use to evaluate employees?
- How do you motivate employees?
- Do you provide training opportunities for employees? If so, what are they?

OA20-2 (Goals 1 and 3)

The student is to rate himself or herself on the leadership instrument give in the Applications Workbook. The student is also to ask a classmate to rate him or her. The student is to write a short report on ways that he or she can improve. The report is not to be submitted to you.

OA20-3 (Goal 2)

The student is given a situation in which a complaint about a performance evaluation is filed with the Human Resources director. The student is to write an evaluation of the appraisal based on the information provided and to include what should or should not have been said or done by the supervisor and make suggestions for improvement. A copy of the evaluation is to be submitted to you. Here are suggested items to be included in the evaluation.

- Always give an employee reasons for evaluating a person "below expectations." A statement such as "Try to do better next year" is not appropriate.
- Don't quote what other employees have said about the employee to the employee. Always deal with the issue; if the statements made are important enough to deal with, find out if they are true. Then talk with the employee about the issue.
- Don't criticize an employee for something done six months previously that you have never mentioned before. Always deal with a problem immediately.
- Never talk about how other people are being evaluated. Evaluations should always be confidential.

- Conduct an evaluation at a time when you have at least an hour to spend with the employee. Conduct the evaluation in a room where others cannot hear. Close the door to the room; do not accept any interruptions (unless urgent, of course). Have your phone calls held until after the evaluation.

  Suggestions for the future include:

- Evaluate performance on a day-to-day basis.
- Allow adequate time for evaluation.
- Give credit to an employee when he or she deserves it; look for something positive to say during the evaluation.
- Be fair.
- Give the person a chance to talk, and answer his or her questions. Do not dismiss the person or his or her questions.
- Avoid personal areas.
- Establish objectives. Help the person improve.

KEY TO ONLINE RESEARCH APPLICATION

ORA20-4 (Goal 2)

The student is to search the home pages of four corporations on the Internet and look for their mission and value statements or company background information that gives information about the corporation's directions and values. A short report of the findings is to be written (with sources identified) and submitted to you.

KEY TO END OF PART 6 ACTIVITIES

Vocabulary Review: Part 6 (Chapters 19–20)

If you are grading these items, each one is worth two points.

1. networking
2. resume
3. portfolio
4. virtual interview
5. follow-up letter
6. performance appraisals
7. commitment
8. exit interview
9. leadership
10. power
11. empowerment
12. long-range planning
13. tactical planning
14. job analysis
15. delegation

Language Skills Practice: Part 6 (Chapters 19–20)

If you are grading these items, each one (including the rules on word division) is worth two points.

1. Our office hours are from 8:30 a.m. to 5 p.m.
2. Dr. J. T. Adams will deliver the commencement address.
3. Reverend Frakes will provide the invocation for the dinner on Tuesday.
4. He observes Yom Kippur, a Jewish holiday.
5. St. Louis and Kansas City are being considered as possible sites for the next convention.
6. Hugh Baker was recently promoted to vice president of Minor Pharmaceuticals.
7. The title of the book is *Procedures for the Office Professional.*
8. The laser printer will cost $500, but the cabinet will be several hundred dollars less.
9. I will see you at 8 a.m. tomorrow.
10. The ratio of lecture hours to laboratory hours for most science courses is 1 to 3.
11. Accept my compliments for a job well done.
12. The temperature was cold much farther south than we expected.
13. Since its record is good, I bought the stock.
14. Only 50 percent of the amount has been paid.
15. The stock list did not include diskettes or stationery.
16. A number of CPAs attended the conference.
17. Her brother-in-law's property joins mine.
18. The people's hopes are optimistic.
19. The speaker said, "The power that moves individuals is enthusiasm."
20. Have you read the article "Ten Tips for the Effective Manager"?
21. What a scene!
22. Did the employment counselor say, "Learn all you can about the company before your interview"?
23. Jill Baugham, the sales associate in your region, will be calling you next week.
24. Louisville, Kentucky, and Knoxville, Tennessee, are all on our itinerary.
25. The last scene of the play depicted an accident in which the main character was lying unconscious in the street.
26. Even though my conscience was clear, I still felt embarrassed to be part of the group.
27. It was as though they had been reprimanded in front of the whole world!
28. radia-tion
    Rule: When two vowels come together within a word, with each vowel sounded separately, divide the word between the vowels.
29. rec-tify
    Rule: Divide words between syllables.
30. moni-tor
    Rule: If a one-letter syllable falls within a word, divide the word after the one-letter syllable.
31. forestall-ing
    Rule: When a base word ends in a double consonant, divide between the base word and the suffix.

ACHIEVEMENT TEST
PART 1 (Chapters 1–4)

PART A—TRUE-FALSE

Directions: The answer to each of the following statements is either true or false. Indicate your choice in the Answers column by circling **T** for a true statement or **F** for a false statement. Each correct answer is worth 1 point.

Answers

F, C1, p. 3   1. By 2020, the Hispanic population is projected to be 10 percent.

T, C1, p. 5   2. The people who make up the workforce today are more diverse than ever before.

T, C1, p. 6   3. The number of women in the workforce is expected to increase to 47 percent by 2006.

F, C1, p. 6   4. The average age of retirement is expected to stay at approximately 65.

T, C1, p. 8   5. A flattened organizational structure has fewer levels than the traditional structure.

T, C2, p. 33   6. Technical skills are important for the project team to work effectively.

F, C2, p. 36   7. Loyalty between the office professional and the employer is unimportant.

T, C2, p. 39   8. One method of dissipating the anger of upset visitors is to allow them to talk.

F, C2, p. 39   9. The origin of the term *grapevine* goes back to World War I.

F, C2, p. 41   10. An autocratic style of management encourages participation among workers.

T, C2, p. 41   11. Openness to multicultural differences is necessary if an individual is to be an effective communicator.

F, C2, p. 46   12. VDTs are considered the occupational illness of the decade.

T, C2, p. 48   13. Substance abuse is prevalent in the workplace.

F, C3, p. 58   14. Chronic stress occurs when a person has to respond instantaneously to a crisis situation.

T, C3, p. 59   15. Job stress costs U.S. businesses billions of dollars each year.

T, C3, p. 64   16. Time management means managing yourself in relation to time.

F, C3, p. 74   17. Electronic time management systems are unable to access stored information.

T, C3, p. 77   18. PIM software allows you to access information stored on the World Wide Web.

F, C4, p. 85   19. Consumers are uninterested in business behaving ethically.

F, C4, p. 86   20. The work ethic that began as a religious teaching in the fourteenth century and was carried to the American colonies is called the Presbyterian Ethic.

T, C4, p. 88   21. The ideas, customs, values, and skills of a particular organization are referred to as organizational culture.

F, C4, p. 91   22. Images held of people or things that are derived from selective perception is referred to as prejudice.

F, C4, p. 93   23. A person lacking in moral judgment is referred to as biased.

PART B—MATCHING

Directions: In the Answers column, write the letter of the item in Column 1 that defines the statement in Column 2. Each correct answer is worth 2 points.

Column 1	*Answers*	*Column 2*
A. ethical behavior	B, C1, p. 4	1. The era technology has spawned
B. digital	H, C1, p. 7	2. A business that operates both within the United States and in countries outside the United States
C. hierarchical		
D. team	C, C1, p. 8	3. A business that is organized according to rank or authority
E. empowerment		
F. role ambiguity	I, C1, p. 12	4. Telecommunication signals going back and forth between individuals at two different locations at the same time
G. time		
H. multinational		
I. synchronously	K, C1, p. 18	5. A unique kind of purposeful thinking in which the thinker systematically chooses conscious and deliberate inquiry
J. values		
K. critical thinking		
L. visualization	D, C2, p. 30	6. A group of individuals who work together to achieve defined goals
M. tact		
N. procrastinator	J, C2, p. 30	7. Principles and qualities that are important to an individual
O. social responsibility		
	E, C2, p. 32	8. Giving the worker access to information needed to do his or her job
	N, C2, p. 36	9. A person who delays in performing tasks
	M, C2, p. 37	10. Skill and grace in dealing with others
	F, C3, p. 60	11. Lack of adequate information about the job and lack of clarity about work objectives and expectations
	L, C3, p. 63	12. Using your imagination to help you relax
	G, C3, p. 64	13. A resource that cannot be bought, sold, rented, borrowed, saved, or manufactured
	O, C4, p. 85	14. The trustworthiness of business to assume accountability for the impact it has on people, the community in which it exists, and the larger world in which it operates
	A, C4, p. 84	15. Doing what is right, not merely what is profitable

PART C—SHORT ANSWER

Directions: For each of the following statements, provide the answers required. The point value is given for each statement. Place your answers on a separate sheet of paper; you may want to use the computer in answering these questions.

1. List six skills needed by the office professional. (12 points) (C1, pp. 17–19)

   The student may list any six of the following:

   - Communication skills
   - Human relations skills
   - Time and organizational management skills
   - Critical thinking skills
   - Decision-making skills
   - Creative thinking skills
   - Technology skills
   - Lifelong-learning skills

2. List and explain five factors that affect ergonomics. (10 points) (C2, pp. 43–45)

   - Color. Color influences the way visitors regard a company as well as the productivity and morale of its employees. Attractive, cheerful, and efficient-looking offices tend to inspire confidence and trust. In contrast, drab or poorly painted offices can arouse doubt or mistrust. Studies have shown that productivity increases and absenteeism decreases as a result of improved color in the office.
   - Lighting. Improper lighting can cause headaches, eye fatigue, neck and shoulder muscle strain, and irritability. If improper lighting conditions continue over a period of time, productivity and morale are lowered, which in turn can cost a business considerable dollars.
   - Acoustics. Sound in the office can be good or bad. Subdued conversations are necessary in the office and do not disrupt the workday. Street sounds and clattering machines can irritate and disturb employees. Noise interferes with communication, makes concentration difficult, and causes irritation and fatigue.
   - Floor plans. The technological revolution demands that floor plans be as flexible as possible. To provide maximum flexibility, office planners are using furnishings that can be easily moved. Flexible furnishings offer the office professional some control over the work environment. The professional has the capability to organize the workspace, within limits, to create a comfortable and pleasant environment.
   - Furniture and Equipment. Much of the office furniture of today is modular. Desktops, shelves, and cabinets attach to partitions, and these units can be adjusted for height, efficiency, and attractiveness. Pneumatically operated ergonomic chairs that are fully adjustable for seat height and tilt, back height and tilt, and arms that are continuously height-adjustable should be purchased. Computers and other technological equipment require that ergonomic factors be considered.

3. List and explain five stress coping techniques. (10 points) (C3, pp. 61–64)

   The student may list and explain any five of the following:

   - Do a stress audit. Make a list of the circumstances that contribute to negative stress. Ask which of the circumstances you can do something about. Prepare a plan of action detailing what you plan to do to decrease stress.
   - Maintain a proper diet. Excessive intake of fat, sugar, salts, and caffeine contributes to poor health and to certain diseases such as hypertension and heart disease.
   - Set up an exercise program. Regular exercise can lower blood pressure, decrease fats in the blood, reduce joint stiffness, lessen appetite, and decrease fatigue.
   - Get the proper amount of sleep. Although the amount of sleep needed varies by each individual, studies have shown that people who sleep seven to eight hours a night tend to live longer than people whose sleep is longer or shorter.
   - Use visualization. Visualization is using your imagination to help you relax. Through visualization, you block out unwanted thoughts.
   - Clarify values. Know what your values are and live by them.
   - Reduce organizational dependency. Do not depend totally on the organization. Educate and train yourself to be employable by a number of organizations.
   - Understand role relationships. Know how you fit into the organizational structure. Accept people; be tolerant; strive to communicate openly and honestly.

4. List and explain five factors that produce ethical change. (15 points) (C4, pp. 94–95)

The student may list and explain any five of the following:

- Determine the ethical change required. Evaluate the situation or situations and determine the change required and the behavior that must be demonstrated.
- Determine the steps required to achieve the objective. Establish criteria and generate possible alternatives to meet the changes needed.
- Practice the new behaviors. Use the new behaviors.
- Seek feedback. Ask friends or trusted advisors to evaluate the behaviors.
- Reward groups and/or individuals. Congratulate people on the effective changes that have been made.
- Evaluate the effects of the ethical change. Determine how the change in the individual or group has impacted the organization, the individual, and/or the group.

PART D—OPTIONAL CASE

Select two of your classmates to work with you on this case. Respond to the items at the end of the case. (20 points)

Karen's supervisor, Dr. Kayes, is president of Marietta College. Dr. Kayes reports directly to a seven-member Board of Trustees. Karen is the administrative assistant to both Dr. Kayes and the Board of Trustees. Her job includes the following:

- Making travel arrangements for the board
- Scheduling special meetings for the board
- Preparing minutes of board meetings
- Making arrangements for dinners for the board

The board members are extremely nice, with the exception of one woman—Carol Crimson. Carol always adopts a condescending attitude when talking with Karen. She will say things such as: "I know you don't have much experience and can't be expected to know the particulars about each situation, but you handled the last situation all wrong," She then proceeds to give Karen advice; however, Karen knows from her conversations with the other board members that they do not agree with her. She consistently asks that Karen violate procedures that the entire board has agreed on. Here are some examples.

- She asks Karen to schedule a limousine to take her to the airport for a board trip; the board procedures state that no one will take a limousine.
- She asks Karen to schedule her in the most expensive rooms on board trips; the board has specifically stated that board members will seek moderate-priced rooms.
- She asks Karen to send her copies of the board minutes the next morning after the board meeting. The board policy is that the minutes go out to everyone within five days after the meeting.
- She asks that Karen order her special meals for board meetings. Although there is no board procedure here, it is more expensive to order special meals.
- She has called Karen several times and stated that she has not received certain materials that Karen is positive that she sent.

She is a board member, and Karen understands that she deserves her respect. However, Karen definitely thinks she is out of line on these issues. At this point, Karen has not crossed her. Karen has done what the board member has asked, but her demands are becoming greater. Karen knows that if she continues to give in to her demands, she is violating board procedure. Karen has not said anything to Dr. Kayes at this point; the latter is extremely busy. Karen feels that she needs to assume as much responsibility as possible.

Answers will vary; here are suggested responses.

What are the issues in this case?

- One board member is demanding services from the office professional that the person is not authorized to perform; the board member's requests are beyond the scope of the office professional's job. Secondarily, a board member is treating the office professional with disrespect.
- Karen, the office professional, seems to understand the importance of giving respect, loyalty, acceptance, and dependability to the employer. However, the office professional is attempting to take too much responsibility. In this case, the office professional

should not accede to the board member's requests. The one exception might be the special food requests if the board member has special dietary or religious considerations. However, Karen should make sure Dr. Kayes is aware of this, if this is the case.

How should the office professional handle the situation?

- She should immediately talk with Dr. Kayes, explaining everything that has happened—the board member's requests and how each request has been handled at this point. Karen must not let the board member browbeat her. When an improper request is made, she should merely say (very politely), "The request is beyond the scope of my responsibility. You may want to talk with the board chairperson about your requests."
- Karen must recognize that she cannot give in to one board member's requests. It is beyond the scope of her responsibility. All requests should be referred immediately to Dr. Kayes in the future. It is Dr. Kayes's responsibility to discuss the matter with the entire board to see what it wants to do.
- As to the mail issue, Karen should devise a procedure to assure that the board member is receiving the mail. She might request a return receipt so that she knows the board member has the packet.

ACHIEVEMENT TEST
PART 2 (Chapters 5–8)

PART A—TRUE-FALSE

Directions: The answer to each of the following statements is either true or false. Indicate your choice in the Answers column by circling **T** for a true statement or **F** for a false statement. Each correct answer is worth 1 point.

Answers

F, C5, p. 114   1. Voice recognition is an output device.

T, C5, p. 114   2. The most frequently used input device is the computer keyboard.

F, C5, p. 115   3. Scanners come in one basic design—flatbed scanners.

F, C5, p. 116   4. A MICR is used by the Postal Service to read keyboarded and handwritten information on envelopes.

F, C5, p. 117   5. Current voice-recognition systems use discrete voice recognition.

T, C5, p. 121   6. Microcomputers are the smallest of the computer systems.

F, C6, p. 143   7. Applications software controls the systems of your computer.

T, C6, p. 148   8. Integrated software is a set of software that typically includes several applications within one program.

T, C6, p. 150   9. A database program helps you store and manipulate data in a manner that allows fast and easy access to it.

T, C6, p. 158   10. Isometric exercise can be done at your desk.

F, C6, p. 159   11. A disk defragmenter controls power fluctuations.

F, C7, p. 169   12. Low-volume copiers typically produce from 25 to 56 copies per minute.

T, C7, p. 171   13. Copier/duplicators can produce volumes of over 50,000 copies monthly.

F, C7, p. 172   14. Copiers can usually handle only one size of paper.

T, C7, p. 174   15. A modem is an electronic device that converts computer signals into telephone signals.

F, C7, p. 181   16. Centralized copy centers are designed to serve the needs of small groups of people and are placed in proximity to the people being served.

F, C7, p. 184   17. It is ethical to use the office copier to copy documents for your personal use.

T, C7, p. 179   18. A maintenance contract may be cost-effective for a copier.

F, C7, p. 183   19. The Copyright Law imposes no restriction on copying materials.

T, C7, p. 186   20. A fax machine sends documents from one location to another via
                            communication networks.

F, C7, p. 183   21. It is illegal to copy any type of information that has a copyright on it.

T, C8, p. 196   22. The number of people who work in a virtual environment is expected
                            to continue to grow.

F, C8, p. 199   23. Working in a virtual environment requires less discipline since you set
                            your own schedule and pace of work.

T, C8, p. 203   24. Isolation is one of the challenges that the virtual worker faces.

T, C8, p. 206   25. When working in a virtual environment, it is important to keep in
                            touch with coworkers who are involved in the same type of projects you are.

T, C8, p. 213   26. Working in a home virtual environment can provide certain tax benefits.

PART B—MATCHING

Directions: In the Answers column, write the letter of the item in Column 1 that defines the statement in Column 2. Each correct answer is worth 2 points.

Column 1	*Answers*	*Column 2*
A. digital	G, C5, p. 118	1. A device that uses a drop-down menu and icons for executing commands and choosing program options
B. shredder		
C. fax-on-demand	J, C5, p. 118	2. A hand-controlled device that operates like a remote control box and allows the user to move the cursor and choose menu commands without using the keyboard
D. bundled software		
E. spreadsheet		
F. reprographics	H, C5, p. 121	3. A single miniature chip that contains the circuitry and components for arithmetic, logic, and control operations
G. GUI		
H. microprocessor	L, C5, p. 123	4. Units of computer memory
I. trackball	O, C5, p. 124	5. A small, portable disk drive
J. mouse	I, C5, p. 118	6. A stationary device that is rolled with the fingers to move the pointer on a computer screen
K. templates		
L. gigabytes	P, C6, p. 144	7. Windows
M. duplexing	D, C6, p. 147	8. Programs that are sold with a computer as part of a combined hardware/software package
N. fax broadcasting		
O. Zip drive	E, C6, p. 149	9. A grid of rows and columns in which you enter numbers and text
P. operating system		
	K, C6, p. 152	10. A predesigned document that contains formatting
	F, C7, p. 169	11. The process of making copies of documents
	A, C7, p. 171	12. Technology that allows data to be transferred as a series of bits rather than as fluctuating signals
	M, C7, p. 173	13. Copying on both sides of the paper
	B, C7, p. 185	14. A machine that cuts paper into strips
	N, C7, p. 187	15. The ability to transmit to multiple locations simultaneously
	C, C7, p. 187	16. The capacity to store information for instant retrieval via fax

PART C—SHORT ANSWER

1. List and explain five types of computer storage devices. (10 points) (C5, pp. 123–126)

   - Floppy disks. Disks (also referred to as diskettes) are indispensable storage mediums for the computer. The size used presently is 3.5 inches. It is housed in a nonremovable, fairly rigid plastic case.
   - Zip disks and drives. A Zip drive is a small, portable disk drive developed primarily to meet the needs of mobile users. It allows for true portability, enabling users to take files and applications anywhere they carry their notebook computers. Each Zip disk holds 100MB of data (the equivalent of 70 floppy disks).
   - Compact disk storage. A compact disk is a storage medium for digital data. The disk is read by an optical scanning mechanism that uses a high-intensity light source, such as a laser and mirrors. Compact disks come in several types, including:
     —CD-ROM
     —CD-R
     —CD-E
     —WORM
     —DVD-ROM
     —DVD-R
     —DVD-AM
   - Hard disks. Hard disks (also called magnetic disks) are secondary storage for mainframe and minicomputers.
   - Magnetic tape. Magnetic tape has been used as a storage medium for mainframe computers for years. Tape can also be a storage medium for minicomputers and microcomputers.

2. List and explain five methods of caring for software. (10 points) (C6, pp. 160 and 162)

   The student may list any five of the following:

   - When labeling a disk, write on the adhesive label before applying it to the disk cover. Remove old labels on a disk before applying a new label.
   - Store the 3.5-inch disk in a specially designed container to keep the disk free of dust and smoke particles.
   - Magnets can erase information on floppy disks, so keep them away from disks. Also, keep paper clips away from disks; paper clips have some magnetic characteristics.
   - Do not store disks close to a telephone. A ringing telephone can create a magnetic field.
   - Keep floppy disks away from water and other liquids. Dry them with a lint-free cloth if they should get wet.
   - Keep floppy disks out of direct sunlight and away from radiators and other sources of heat.
   - Write-protect a disk if it contains data that you do not want changed.
   - Educate yourself about computer viruses.
   - Make backups of files immediately—before you have a virus.
   - Download only from sources you trust.
   - Install an antiviral scanning program.
   - Do not allow programs to be loaded on your system without your authorization.
   - Purchase all software programs in tamper-proof packaging.
   - Always boot from a write-protected disk.
   - When you get a new program, write-protect the master disk before inserting it into a drive.

3. List ten special features that are available on copiers. (10 points) (C7, pp. 173–176)

   The student may list any ten of the following:

   - Reduction and enlargement
   - Duplexing
   - Color reproduction
   - Document or digital editing
   - Diagnostics
   - Collate and staple
   - Interrupt key
   - Help button
   - Job recovery
   - Automatic folding
   - Touch control screen

- Programmable memory
- Book copy
- Online binding
- Image shift
- Transparency production
- Toner and paper changes
- Environmentally friendly features such as organic photoconductors, recyclable materials, toner-save modes, and energy-save modes

4. Identify and explain six personality traits essential for the successful virtual worker. (12 points) (C8, pp. 199–202)

The student may identify any six of the following:

- Disciplined. Working in a virtual home or away from the traditional office means that there are a number of distractions. Discipline is essential to set a routine, establish times to communicate with the office, and let the family or friends know when you are working and cannot be disturbed.
- Self-Starter. A self-starter knows what needs to be done and is anxious to get it done. The self-starter generally has numerous items on his or her to-do list and not only gets them accomplished, but feels a real sense of satisfaction as he or she is able to mark the items off the list. Being a self-starter in a virtual environment means that the work gets done.
- Organized. Organization is always important on the job, but it is particularly important in a virtual situation. If an individual is to juggle numerous tasks and successfully confront numerous interruptions, the person must be organized. Organization means, among other things, the ability to set priorities, organize the workstation, simplify repetitive work, handle paperwork as few times as possible, and use time management systems.
- Creative. In the traditional office situation, you generally have someone you can go to for help in solving a particular problem or situation. Not so in a virtual environment. You have to be a creative problem solver.
- Good communicator. Good communication skills are crucial to the virtual worker. He or she must communicate with a variety of people (executives, coworkers, clients, employees at the local print shop, and so forth). The virtual worker generally does not have the luxury of communicating with these people on a daily basis, which means that good communication skills are doubly important. First impressions are many times lasting impressions.
- Energetic. The virtual worker must be energetic. There is no one to set the time clock, no one to determine the length of breaks or lunchtime. The virtual worker must be able to set and maintain a schedule that allows the work to get done, even if it means burning the midnight oil on occasion.
- Self-confident. The virtual worker needs to know himself or herself well. When something is done well, the virtual worker needs to take the time to congratulate himself or herself. The virtual worker has to have the self-confidence to be his or her own support system.

PART D—OPTIONAL CASE

Select two of your classmates to work with you on this case. Respond to the items at the end of the case. (20 points)

Edward has worked for McLean Services for two years. He enjoys his job and consistently has received excellent performance evaluations. He gets along well with his coworkers, and they like him. A month ago, the company vice president's daughter was hired to work in the same department where Edward works. She seems like a nice enough person, but Edward thinks she is making several mistakes. The second week that she was on the job, Edward saw her copying some personal information. Edward knows that she is taking a course in the evening, and he thought she was probably copying the information for her class. However, he did mention to her that the company policy states that employees cannot copy for personal use. She said that it was not personal, but it was for a professional organization to which she belongs. Edward thinks it is still questionable, but he did not say anything else. Yesterday, he walked into her area and noticed that she was copying a software package. He didn't say anything, since he had tried to talk with her before and she ignored him. Edward has heard that several years ago a person was fired for copying a software package. He wonders why the boss's daughter is receiving special treatment. He has also noticed several little things—she is always late coming back from lunch. Also, she is often late for work or leaves early. Other employees in the department have made remarks to Edward about the special treatment that she is receiving. After thinking about it overnight, Edward is upset. He doesn't think that the boss's daughter should be allowed to behave unethically.

The answers will vary; here are suggested responses.

What are the issues in the case?

- The case suggests that Edward lives by a set of values. Edward is offended because he believes the boss's daughter is behaving unethically and being allowed to get away with that behavior. He also does not believe the supervisor is being fair. According to the rumor mill, a previous employee was fired for such behavior. Edward believes that unethical behavior should always be punished. In other words, Edward's values have been violated.

Should Edward ignore the situation or speak out? If so, to whom should he talk and how should he frame the issue?

- Edward should first of all speak to the boss's daughter again and let her know that it is illegal to copy software. If she responds that she did not know it was, he should reaffirm that it is. Then he should assume at this point that she will not do it again. If she denies ever doing it and he is certain that it did occur, he should discuss the "perceived violation" with his supervisor. However, he should present the case as a "perceived violation"—not as a certainty. He should tell his supervisor that he wants to be clear about the company policy and that he believes it is important that policy be upheld. The topic is an extremely sensitive one, but Edward should not give away his values. Edward might also ask the supervisor if the copier can be used to make copies for a professional organization. At this point, he should not accuse the boss's daughter of making copies for her class. He has no proof. If she continues to make copies that are personal, Edward might say something—but not at this point. Edward must remember that he is not the supervisor and even though things do not seem right to him, he could be wrong. Edward also should not say to the supervisor that he has heard that another employee was fired for such an action; the information is hearsay. Edward has no proof. Edward wants to come across as a person who cares about the company and its policies. He also wants to let the supervisor know that ethical behavior is extremely important. Edward does not want to appear as a gossip or someone who is trying to usurp the supervisor's role. However, if the supervisor ignores the software copying situation and there is other unethical behavior occurring in the department, Edward may want to ask for a transfer to another department or begin looking for another job. He will probably be uncomfortable working in an environment where his values and the values of the company do not match.

ACHIEVEMENT TEST
PART 3 (Chapters 9–13)

PART A—TRUE-FALSE

Directions: The answer to each of the following statements is either true or false. Indicate your choice in the Answers column by circling **T** for a true statement or **F** for a false statement. Each correct answer is worth 1 point.

Answers

T, C9, p. 223   1. Your self-concept is built in part on how others see and respond to you.

F, C9, p. 224   2. There is no connection between speech and voice patterns and self-image.

T, C9, p. 230   3. The study of the personal and cultural use of space is called territoriality.

F, C9, p. 229   4. Time is a nonverbal communicator.

T, C9, p. 234   5. Categorization is the ability to compare, contrast, and classify objects, persons, or ideas.

F, C9, p. 235   6. Studies show that people spend 50 percent of their time communicating.

T, C10, p. 245   7. When preparing written correspondence, it is important to understand who the reader(s) will be.

F, C10, p. 251   8. Effective paragraphs are written in the passive voice.

F, C10, p. 253   9. It is less important to pay attention to grammar when writing an email than when writing a letter.

T, C10, p. 253   10. It is acceptable to use "emoticons" when composing email correspondence.

T, C10, p. 254   11. Legal action information should not be sent by email.

T, C10, p. 258   12. Persuasive messages attempt to get the reader to take some action.

T, C11, p. 271   13. With a block-style letter, all lines begin at the left margin.

F, C11, p. 273   14. MIRs are used by the U.S. Postal Service to scan envelopes.

T, C11, p. 270   15. Mixed punctuation includes a colon after the salutation and a comma after the complimentary close.

T, C11, p. 275   16. Quotations may be documented in reports by using the MLA format.

T, C11, p. 281   17. In a document, quotations of fewer than four lines are included in the body of the report and enclosed in quotation marks.

T, C11, p. 284   18. When delivering a presentation, you should use the active voice rather than the passive voice.

F, C13, p. 330   19. The fastest mail service available through the United States Postal Service is priority mail.

F, C13, p. 331   20. Registered mail is available for all types of mail.

T, C13, p. 331   21. Standard Mail (A) consists of mail weighing less than 16 ounces.

F, C13, p. 332   22. COD means "cash on delivery" and allows the mailer to collect the price of goods and/or postage on the items delivered.

T, C13, p. 332   23. Certified mail is used for materials that have no monetary value but for which a record of delivery is needed.

T, C13, p. 335   24. Some private mail companies provide services through the Internet.

T, C13, p. 338   25. No punctuation is used when addressing envelopes to be read by OCR machines.

F, C13, p. 342   26. Confidential mail should be opened by the office professional and placed in a special folder for the executive.

PART B—MATCHING

Directions: In the Answers column, write the letter of the item in Column 1 that defines the statement in Column 2. Each correct answer is worth 2 points.

Column 1	*Answers*	*Column 2*
A. analogies	E, C9, p. 223	1. The ability to make known information, thought, or feeling so that it is adequately understood
B. executive		
C. readability	F, C9, p. 223	2. The way you see yourself
D. encoding	D, C9, p. 227	3. The process of turning an idea into symbols that can be communicated
E. communication		
F. self-concept	I, C10, p. 251	4. A structure in which grammatically equivalent forms are used within a sentence
G. fax		
H. you approach	C, C10, p. 252	5. The degree of difficulty of the message
I. parallelism	H, C10, p. 257	6. A concept in which the writer places the reader at the center of the message
J. bar code		
K. annotating	L, C10, p. 257	7. A concept in which the writer attempts to place himself or herself in the shoes of the reader
L. empathy		
	B, C10, p. 262	8. A short summary of the written report
	A, C11, p. 284	9. Comparing two different things by stressing the similarities between the two
	G, C13, p. 336	10. An electronic message
	K, C13, p. 344	11. Underlining important elements of a piece of correspondence
	J, C13, p. 337	12. One of the sorters used by the United States Postal Service

PART C—SHORT ANSWER

1. Define "allness" and "inference" and explain how each impacts communication. (4 points) (C9, pp. 232–233)

   Allness is a communication problem that occurs when an individual presumes that what he or she says or knows is complete, absolute, and all-inclusive. People may take different details from a given situation and assume that each individual person knows all there is to know. When the people begin to talk, there is a tremendous communication problem since assumptions have been made that are not true.

   Inference is defined as the process of deriving logical conclusions from premises known or assumed to be true. Inference impacts communication when individuals act on the inference. The first step in correcting inference problems is to be aware that you may be making an inference. It is essential to know the difference between an inference and an observation.

2. List and explain four ways that communication barriers may be reduced. (8 points) (C9, pp. 235–236)

   - Active listening. Active listening requires that you listen for the meaning as well as the words of the speaker. To become an active listener, prepare to listen, listen for facts, listen for feelings, minimize blocks and filters, and question and paraphrase.
   - Person oriented. Be sensitive to what the words in a communication mean to the receiver of the communication.
   - Nonjudgmental. Do not attempt to judge an individual's intelligence, appearance, or any other characteristics. Give the person a chance to get his or her message across without forming judgments.
   - Conflict resolution. When conflicts occur, use conflict resolution techniques such as:
     —Acknowledge the work of the other person
     —Acknowledge the other person's emotions and feelings
     —Agree with the other person's point of view when possible
     —Express your point of view without denigrating the other person
     —Acknowledge differences openly
     —Ask for the other person's advice
     —Build bridges between differences rather than walls that restrict

3. Describe five characteristics of effective written correspondence. (10 points) (C10, pp. 245–247)

   The student may describe any five of the following:

   - Complete. Correspondence is complete if it gives the reader all the information needed to accomplish the results the writer intends.
   - Clear. After reading a message, the reader should be able to determine without a doubt the purpose of the correspondence.
   - Accurate. Get the facts before you start to write. Check your information carefully.
   - Prompt. Prompt answers to messages say to the readers that the writer or company cares about them.
   - Concise. Conciseness in writing means expressing the necessary information in as few words as possible.
   - Courteous. Courteousness in correspondence means using good human relations skills as you write. Treat the reader with respect; write as if you care about the reader.
   - Positive. Using a positive tone will give the reader a favorable association with the writer, the company, and/or the product. A positive tone is set by the words chosen and the way they are used.

4. Describe six steps you should take in preparing oral presentations. (12 points) (C11, pp. 282–287)

   The student may list any six of the following steps:

   - Determine the purpose
   - Determine the anticipated audience
   - Determine the setting
   - Gather the material
   - Organize the presentation
   - Develop an opening
   - Use powerful language
   - Develop a strong closing
   - Pay attention to body language
   - Use visual aids
   - Dress appropriately
   - Rehearse the presentation
   - Control nervousness
   - Critique the presentation

5. List eight effective telephone techniques. (16 points) (C12, pp. 310–314)

   The student may list any eight of the following:

   - Develop a pleasant voice
   - Speak distinctly
   - Be helpful and discreet
   - Ask questions tactfully
   - Take messages completely and accurately
   - Be attentive
   - Avoid slang
   - Use the caller's name
   - Transfer calls properly
   - Terminate calls courteously
   - Keep a list of frequently called numbers
   - Handle problem calls

PART D—OPTIONAL CASE

Select two of your classmates to work with you on this case. Respond to the items at the end of the case. (20 points)

Carmen has been employed as an office professional by Spectrum Health for three months. When she was employed, two of the other office professionals (Sandra and Judith) were extremely friendly with her. They invited her to lunch several times; she went with them and enjoyed their company. On the occasions when Carmen has gone out to lunch with the two, Judith and Sandra have talked openly about several coworkers that they have dated over the years—both have been employed by the company for more than three years. They also suggested to Carmen that there is one man in the office who might be interested in her. However, Carmen made no comment when the statement was made; Carmen is not interested in having a relationship with a coworker. Judith also has invited her to a party at her home; Carmen was unable to go due to a conflict. Carmen prefers not to become best friends with either person. She is concerned that it may interfere with their working relationship.

Carmen is very cordial to both Judith and Sandra. Recently, she has noticed both of them are very cold to her. And one of the other office professionals told her that Sandra is spreading rumors about Carmen—that she is having an affair with one of the men in the office. The coworker also told her that she should have nothing to do with either person—both are trouble. Judith has made several negative comments to Carmen's face, one being, "Everyone thinks you can do no wrong, but I know that isn't true." (Carmen's supervisor has complimented her work several times, and Carmen assumes that Judith overheard the supervisor's remarks.) Other remarks include such statements as, "You look dowdy today," and "Something needs to be done with your hair; let me take you to my hairdresser." Carmen dresses very conservatively; Judith dresses in a manner that Carmen considers inappropriate for the office—lots of jewelry, extremely short skirts, and heavy makeup. Carmen does not understand what has happened. Carmen is a relatively private person and seldom discusses her personal life with coworkers. She is concerned about the situation, but does not know why it has happened and has no clue of what to do about it.

What communication barriers seem to be present?

- Allness. Judith and Sandra have assumed that they know everything about Carmen and have made assumptions on those bases. Actually, they know very little about Carmen. She is a very private person and has not chosen to share her feelings with them.
- Inference. Judith and Sandra have inferred from Carmen's silence that she is interested in a relationship with a man—the man they suggested to her and then they have started a rumor about an affair.
- Categorization. Both Judith and Sandra have categorized Carmen based on her gender and age. They have made assumptions on these bases—assumptions that fit their mold, not Carmen's. For example, Judith has determined that Carmen needs help in dressing since she doesn't dress in the same manner that Judith does. In actuality, Carmen does not believe Judith is dressing appropriately.

What can be done to reduce them?

In order to resolve the problem, these steps need to be taken to reduce the communication barriers.

- Active listening
- Nonjudgmental behavior
- Conflict resolution

Develop a plan of action for Carmen in dealing with both Judith and Sandra.

- Using conflict resolution techniques, Carmen should talk with Sandra about the affair rumor. Let Sandra know what she has heard, and ask Sandra if she knows how the rumor could have started. After all, it is a rumor; Carmen does not know that Sandra started it. Carmen should listen for feelings as Sandra talks, minimize her own mental blocks and filters, and question and paraphrase when Sandra makes statements. Carmen should make it very clear to Sandra that her (Carmen's) value system means that she is not interested in dating a coworker in her same department. She feels it can lead to problems on the job. She should also make it clear to Sandra that she is concerned about the rumor and wants it stopped immediately since there is no truth to it.
- Carmen should continue to be very cordial to both Judith and Sandra; however, she should limit her lunches with them. It would be better to go to lunch occasionally with the office group (including Judith and Sandra) but not with Judith and Sandra by themselves. Carmen should not get into private discussions with either person.
- If Judith continues to make remarks to Carmen about her appearance, Carmen should thank Judith but let her know in a firm but pleasant manner that she pays careful attention to her appearance and intends to make a conservative statement in the way she dresses. Again, Carmen should be definite in her discussion with Judith but not confrontational about Judith's dress and appearance.
- If Judith continues to make remarks to Carmen such as "You can do no wrong," Carmen should just smile and return the statement with a remark such as "Certainly I can." Most of all, she should not let Judith pull her into a conversation about her competence. The problem is Judith's—not Carmen's. Carmen should not try to correct Judith's behavior; she will not be able to do so.

ACHIEVEMENT TEST
PART 4 (Chapters 14–15)

PART A—TRUE-FALSE

Directions: The answer to each of the following statements is either true or false. Indicate your choice in the Answers column by circling **T** for a true statement or **F** for a false statement. Each correct answer is worth 1 point.

Answers

F, C14, p. 359   1. Records management is the systematic control of records over a period of five years.

F, C14, p. 359   2. Records have no legal value.

T, C14, p. 361   3. ARMA has set forth rules for filing.

T, C14, p. 369   4. An alphabetic storage method is an indirect method.

T, C14, p. 378   5. A disadvantage of a geographic storage method is that reference to a card file is often necessary.

T, C14, p. 371   6. One of the advantages of a subject system is that like records are grouped together.

T, C14, p. 372   7. A disadvantage of a subject system is that preparation of materials for the file takes longer than other methods.

T, C14, p. 373   8. A numeric storage system includes an alphabetic general file.

F, C14, p. 375   9. One of the disadvantages of a numeric storage system is that there is limited expansion.

F, C14, p. 375   10. A chronologic storage system is an arrangement in which records are stored with the most recent date last.

T, C14, p. 387   11. Movable-aisle systems take less space than standard file cabinets.

F, C15, p. 394   12. Microimage is the main storage medium for business records.

T, C15, p. 395   13. Information in an automated system may be keyed, scanned, or input through a voice-recognition system.

T, C15, p. 395   14. With a database management system, the user can organize, enter, process, index, sort, select, link related files, store, and retrieve information.

F, C15, p. 396   15. If you are working with a database in a human resources department and entering employee information, the primary key or keyword could be the employee's department name.

T, C15, p. 398   16. When setting up a decentralized electronic filing system, you must determine how you will file the disks or tapes and the naming system and standards that will be used to store any documents.

T, C15, p. 400   17. Computer-generated documents such as memos, faxes, email, bills, and invoices are often called "unstructured data" because they cannot be reduced to fields and records that are stored in a traditional relational database.

F, C15, p. 400   18. The average cost of retrieving a misfiled document is about $20.

F, C15, p. 404   19. Microfiche is a roll containing a series of frames or images much like a movie film.

T, C15, p. 410   20. Although original COLD technology stored information on laser disks, updates to the technology allow the user to store information using a variety of formats including networks, CDs, optical disks, DVDs, or the Internet.

PART B—MATCHING

Directions: In the Answers column, write the letter of the item in Column 1 that defines the statement in Column 2. Each correct answer is worth 2 points.

Column 1	*Answers*	*Column 2*
A. document imaging	F, C15, p. 398	1. System where computers are linked together through a network and files on the network can be accessed by more than one person at a time
B. database		
C. computer-output microfilm (COM)	E, C15, p. 407	2. Plain language data on microfilm are converted into computer-readable data for use in a computer
D. indexing		
E. computer-input microfilm (CIM)	H, C15, p. 401	3. Prevents any alteration to an original document once it is converted to an image
F. centralized storage	B, C15, p. 395	4. A collection of records organized in related files
G. DVD	A, C15, p. 400	5. The practice of converting paper documents to digital format that can be stored on a variety of media and retrieved electronically
H. WORM technology		
I. coding		
J. sorting	J, C14, p. 381	6. Arrangement of materials in the order in which they are to be filed.
K. storing		
	G, C15, p. 402	7. A storage medium that has 7–28 times the storage capacity of current CDs
	C, C15, p. 407	8. When computer documents are produced on microforms rather than paper
	D, C14, p. 380	9. Process of determining where a piece of correspondence is to be stored
	I, C14, p. 380	10. Process of marking the units of the filing segment by which the record is to be stored

PART C—INDEXING

Directions: Select the first, second, and third indexing units for each of the following names. Write the unit on the lines provided to the right of each name. Each indexing unit identified is worth 1 point.

	First Unit	Second Unit	Third Unit
1.	1411	Hill	Street (C14, p. 364)
2.	Kiwanis	Club	Southfield (C14, p. 364)
3.	Mission	Fence	Abilene (C14, p. 364)
4.	Cascade	Township	Kent (T, C14, p. 366)
5.	Wm.	Samuel	Cornelius (C14, p. 362)
6.	Thomas	Company	The (C14, p. 361)
7.	Eastwest	Tennis	Club (C14, p. 362)
8.	X	Y	Z (C14, p. 362)
9.	McCall	Maurice	III (C14, p. 363)
10.	Uncle	Jims	Car (C14, p. 363)

PART D—SHORT ANSWER

Directions: For each of the following statements, provide the answers required. The point value is given for each statement. Place your answers on a separate sheet of paper; you may want to use the computer in answering these questions.

1. Explain the purpose of a cross-reference. (2 points) (C14, p. 380)

   A cross-reference allows you to find correspondence that may be called for under two or more names.

2. What are the advantages of a geographic filing method? List three organizations that might use such a filing method. (8 points) (C14, pp. 377–378)

   Advantages include:
   • It provides for grouping of records by location.
   • The volume of records within any given geographic area can be seen by glancing at the files.
   • It allows for direct filing if the location is known.
   • All the advantages of alphabetic filing are inherent in this method since it is basically an alphabetic arrangement.

   Organizations that may use a geographic file include:
   • Utility companies
   • Real estate firms
   • Sales organizations
   • Government agencies that file by geographic divisions

3. Explain the most likely name to be used for filing on incoming letters and on outgoing letters. (4 points) (C14, p. 380)

   Incoming—the name in the letterhead
   Outgoing—the name in the inside address

4. List five features of a document management software system. (10 points) (C15, p. 400)

   The student may list any five of the following:

   • Log in documents
   • Print file labels
   • Track active files, inactive files, vital records, and off-premise storage
   • Provide an inventory of all records
   • Follow up on overdue files
   • Track nonpaper documents such as disks and microforms
   • Generate activity reports by department and user
   • Generate records retention and disposal guidelines

5. List three advantages of document management systems. (6 points) (C15, p. 403)

   The student may list any three of the following:

   • Electronically filed documents decrease the amount of necessary filing space. With this decrease in used space, the organization can reallocate traditional filing space for other uses.
   • Organizations can increase productivity of employees by eliminating or reducing the amount of time employees will spend storing, retrieving, or tracking documents.
   • Increased retrieval speed is also a major benefit. In addition to improved customer relations, increased access speed helps cut costs by reducing the need for additional staffing to handle growth or seasonal surges in volume.
   • Electronically filed documents do not need to be removed from their filing location, which will decrease or eliminate the possibility of missing documents.
   • Using multiple indexes, documents residing anywhere in the system can be easily found by users. In addition, electronically filed documents can be accessed by multiple users concurrently.

PART E—OPTIONAL CASE

Directions: Select two of your classmates to work with on this case. Respond to the items at the end of the case. (20 points)

Mr. Lu Liang, Records Manager, plans to revise the partial manual and partial automated records management system that are now being used by People First International to a totally automated system. Person Power Corporation, a company with a similar structure to People First, has an automated system that is working well for them. Mr. Liang has talked with the records manager of Person Power and has been invited to spend some time at the facility observing the system. Person Power's home office is in New York City. Stephanie Tolley, the administrative assistant to Mr. Liang, has been with People First for five years and is an extremely knowledgeable and competent individual. Mr. Liang wants her opinion on the system, so he has invited her to go to New York with him. He plans to spend three days in observing the system and talking with the Person Power manager about implementation procedures. Stephanie was pleased when she was invited; she has an interest in automated systems and believes that People First could do a much better job than it is doing presently in records management. She readily accepted the invitation. Although she did not tell any of her coworkers that she was going, she has heard from a good friend in another department that word is going around the office that she and Mr. Liang will be engaged in more than just business during the trip. It is a vicious rumor. The individuals who are allegedly spreading the rumor are coworkers; one is male and one is female. Stephanie considers them her professional colleagues and has never had any problems with them (at least to her knowledge). Stephanie is happily married; her husband feels that the trip is a wonderful professional opportunity for her. She will have a chance to learn more about an area that she is extremely interested in and use her knowledge in helping People First move their records management system forward. She knows little of Mr. Liang's personal life, but she does understand that he is not married. They have worked together for five years, and there has never been any unprofessional conduct on either individual's part. Stephanie is very upset about the rumor; she doesn't know whether or not Mr. Liang has heard it.

Stephanie believes she has at least four options:

- Ignore the rumor
- Talk with the parties involved in spreading the rumor
- Talk with Mr. Liang and get his advice
- Refuse to go on the trip

What course of action would you suggest that Stephanie take? Explain how she should handle whatever course of action you suggest.

Answers will vary; here are suggested responses.

Stephanie should talk with Mr. Liang first and tell him that the rumor is going around. If he feels it is serious enough, he may choose to check it out and talk with the individuals (since they report to him). If he considers it idle gossip that is not harmful to the organization at this point, he may choose to ignore it. Stephanie can choose to talk with the individuals (since they are her colleagues). However, if she does so, she must not accuse them; she should approach it by telling them that she has heard the rumor and she wonders if they know anything about it. She should explain that she is going on a professional trip and she is concerned that anything would be said that would suggest otherwise. If they respond that they have heard nothing, she should thank them for listening to her and ask that if they do hear something they let her know. She should not act overly concerned and should keep the conversation on a very professional level—merely explaining the situation. Stephanie should not refuse to go on the trip. When Mr. Liang and Stephanie return from the trip, there should be a session with the workgroup to tell them about what they have learned and the future directions of the records management group. It also might be a good idea to have a meeting with the workgroup before they go explaining the interest in establishing a completely automated system and the importance of looking at one that is working. Information is power, and the more information people have about an issue, the less likely the possibility of rumors circulating.

ACHIEVEMENT TEST
PART 5 (Chapters 16–18)

Directions: The answer to each of the following statements is either true or false. Indicate your choice in the Answers column by circling **T** for a true statement or **F** for a false statement. Each correct answer is worth 1 point.

PART A—TRUE-FALSE

Answers

F, C16, p. 421	1.	It is appropriate to have a meeting to discuss confidential or sensitive personnel matters.
T, C16, p. 426	2.	In meetings, participants have a responsibility to be nonjudgmental of others' comments.
F, C16, p. 426	3.	A participant has no responsibility once the meeting is over.
T, C16, p. 429	4.	Videoconferencing may be transmitted from a personal computer.
F, C16, p. 432	5.	It is appropriate to use hand gestures in conferences that are international in nature.
T, C16, p. 433	6.	Meeting objectives should be shared with participants before the meeting.
F, C16, p. 434	7.	It is the responsibility of the executive to prepare the meeting agenda.
F, C16, p. 434	8.	Any background materials should be given to attendees during the meeting.
T, C16, p. 440	9.	The administrative assistant should be familiar with parliamentary procedure.
F, C16, p. 442	10.	Minutes should be completed within five days of the meeting.
T, C17, p. 457	11.	When traveling coach on an airline, travelers will find the seats closer together and fewer airline attendants.
F, C17, p. 458	12.	Membership in an airline club is usually free.
T, C17, p. 463	13.	A passport is valid for ten years from the date of issue.
T, C17, p. 464	14.	By July 2002, the Euro will displace national currencies in a variety of countries in Europe.
F, C17, p. 469	15.	Travel agencies are paid by their customers.
T, C17, p. 472	16.	Traveler's checks must be signed at the time of purchase.
T, C18, p. 484	17.	Online debit cards require the use of a PIN to initiate the transaction.
F, C18, p. 485	18.	When a smart card is used only for a specific purpose, it is considered an open system.
F, C18, p. 487	19.	The person or business who orders the bank to pay cash from an account is called the payee.
T, C18, p. 492	20.	Most banks do not return checks but use check truncation.
T, C18, p. 496	21.	Current liabilities are debts that must be paid within one year.
T, C18, p. 498	22.	The Fair Labor Standards Act requires that companies keep a record of hours worked and pay a minimum wage.
F, C18, p. 499	23.	Under the Tax Reform Act of 1985, everyone age 12 or older must have a social security number.
F, C18, p. 501	24.	A personal property tax is levied on land and buildings.

PART B—MATCHING

Directions: In the Answers column, write the letter of the item in Column 1 that defines the statement in Column 2. Each correct answer is worth 2 points.

Column 1	*Answers*	*Column 2*
A. certified check	L, C16, p. 433	1. A group having dissimilar backgrounds and experiences
B. passport	C, C16, p. 433	2. A group with similar backgrounds and experiences
C. homogenous	R, C16, p. 433	3. The ideas and products of a group of people developed through interaction with each other
D. kiosk		
E. circular	F, C16, p. 436	4. An outline of procedures or the order of business to be followed during a meeting
F. agenda		
G. Euro	O, C16, p. 438	5. A room arrangement that is the most effective in formal meetings
H. blank endorsement		
I. jet lag	E, C16, p. 438	6. A room arrangement that works best when the purpose of the meeting is to generate ideas
J. visa		
K. airline clubs	K, C17, p. 458	7. Members usually have access to special airport lounges, current periodicals and newspapers, complimentary soft drinks or juice
L. heterogeneous		
M. ATMs		
N. cashier's check	I, C17, p. 462	8. Medical condition that results in prolonged periods of fatigue
O. rectangular		
P. itinerary	B, C17, p. 463	9. Official government document that certifies the identity and citizenship of an individual and grants the person permission to travel abroad
Q. endorsement in full		
R. synergy		
S. smart cards	G, C17, p. 464	10. Standard currency that will be used in a variety of European countries by July 2002.
	P, C17, p. 466	11. A listing of travel arrangements that includes appointments, hotel reservations, and flight information
	J, C17, p. 463	12. Permits a traveler to enter and travel within a particular country
	D, C18, p. 484	13. Sophisticated equipment that may include interactive video, telephone, electronic capture of signatures, and imaging
	S, C18, p. 485	14. Cash is accepted by machines and converted to stored value
	Q, C18, p. 490	15. Transfers check ownership to another person or business
	M, C18, p. 483	16. Allow a customer to obtain cash, make deposits, transfer funds, and pay for purchases without going to a bank
	H, C18, p. 490	17. Requires only the signature of the payee and makes the check payable to any holder
	A, C18, p. 493	18. A business or personal check that is guaranteed by the bank on which it is drawn
	N, C18, p. 493	19. Check issued by a bank and drawn on the bank's own funds

PART C—SHORT ANSWER

Directions: For each of the following statements, provide the answers required. The point value is given for each statement. Place your answers on a separate sheet of paper; you may want to use the computer in answering these questions.

1. List and explain five roles of the meeting leader. (5 points) (C16, pp. 422–425)

   The student may choose any five of the following:

   - Make the purpose and objectives clear. The leader does not necessarily establish the purpose; he or she determines what the purpose is before the meeting and makes the purpose clear in writing. It is the leader's responsibility to reiterate the purpose at the beginning of the meeting. The leader should also let the participants know the objectives of the meeting—what must be accomplished at the meeting, what needs to be done after the meeting.
   - Adhere to the agenda. The leader must keep the participants focused on the agenda. If participants stray from the agenda, the leader is responsible for sensitively but firmly bringing them back to it.
   - Manage time. The leader is responsible for beginning and ending the meeting on time. Time frames should be established when the notice of the meeting is sent out; the leader is responsible for maintaining these time frames.
   - Encourage participation. Once the meeting begins, the leader is responsible for seeing that all individuals participate. The leader should let the participants know that their opinions are valued and should make it easy for them to participate.
   - Lead a balanced and controlled discussion. The leader should:
     —Keep the participants focused on the agenda
     —Encourage participation from everyone
     —Limit the domination of any one person
     —Positively reinforce all individuals for their contributions
     —Keep the discussion moving toward the objectives and outcomes determined
   - Handle conflict. In order to handle conflict, the leader should:
     —Make the role of the participants clear at the beginning of the meeting; state that conflict will be addressed using conflict resolution techniques.
     —Clarify communication barriers if a conflict arises. Ask that participants define their terms if they are not clear to the group.
     —Concentrate on building a team with the group; stress collaboration rather than competition.
   - Bring closure to the objectives. Ask such questions as, "How are we going to meet this objective?" "What steps will be taken?"
   - Evaluate the meeting. Generally, with informal meetings within the organization, no formal evaluation is done; however, an informal evaluation by the leader and possibly the participants should be done. Here are some questions that can be asked.
     —Were the attendees participatory?
     —Was the nonverbal behavior positive?
     —Were the participants creative problem solvers?
     —Did the participants exhibit a high energy level?
     —Was the purpose of the meeting satisfied?
     —Were appropriate decisions made?
     —Can I improve on how I handled the issues, the people, or the meeting in general?

2. List three advantages and three disadvantages of electronic meetings. (9 points) (C19, p. 431)

   Advantages

   - Savings in travel costs, travel time, meals, and hotel rooms
   - Ability to present a considerable amount of information concisely through sophisticated audio and video technology
   - Ability to bring together people with expertise in a number of different areas to discuss problems of mutual concern with a minimum of effort.
   - Ability to provide information from the conference to individuals who are not in attendance at the conference
   - Ability to be an environmental savings in less pollution of air through cars, planes, and trains

   Disadvantages

   - Less spontaneity between individuals due to a fairly structured environment
   - More formal in nature
   - Inability to see body language of all participants at any one time; inability to pick up small nuances of body language over the monitor
   - Relatively small amount of or no socialization time between participants
   - Less chance for effective brainstorming on issues

3. List three of the items that must be presented to an authorized agent in order to obtain a passport. (6 points) (C17, p. 463)

The student may list any three of the following:

- A completed application
- Proof of United States citizenship through a certified copy of a birth certificate, baptismal certificate, or certificate of naturalization
- Proof of identification through such documents as a valid driver's license, government or military ID, or a previous U.S. passport
- Two identical $2'' \times 2''$ photographs
- The passport fee

4. List five types of information you should have if you are scheduling the executive to travel by air. (5 points) (C17, p. 466)

The student may list five of the following:

- Preferred airlines if he or she has one, along with his or her frequent flyer number.
- Class of flight—first class, business class, or coach
- Preference as to aisle or window seat
- Special food preferences (low-calorie meal, low-cholesterol meal, salt-free meal, and any other special needs)
- Ticket delivery—are tickets to be picked up at the airport, sent by courier, mailed, or delivered by a travel agent?
- Timeline for arriving at the airport
- Corporate policies regarding air travel

5. List four advantages to direct payroll depositing. (4 points) (C18, p. 486)

The student may list any four of the following:

- Eliminates time and expense of writing paychecks for the employer
- Lowers security measures needed in processing and distributing vouchers as opposed to checks for employers
- Reduces postage for employers by not mailing checks
- Decreases the possible loss or theft of paychecks for both employers and employees
- Convenient for employees
- Provides for deposit even when employee is on vacation

6. List the four steps that should be followed when writing checks. (4 points) (C18, pp. 487–488)

Students should list the following four steps:

- The check voucher, stub, or register should be filled out first with the date, amount, and purpose of the check.
- The date should be entered in the space provided on the check.
- The name of the payee should be written in full and as far as possible to the left in the space provided.
- The amount of the check must be written twice. It is first written in figures after the dollar sign. The figures should be placed as close as possible to the printed dollar sign so that no additional figures can be inserted. The amount of the check is then written on the following line with the words for the dollar amount and figures for the cents. Express cents in fractions of 100.

PART D—OPTIONAL CASE

Directions: Select two of your classmates to work with on this case. Respond to the items at the end of the case. (20 points)

Charley Eggers is employed in the human resources department of People First International. One of the goals he and his supervisor set for him this year is to set up and lead a monthly meeting of all office professionals at his company's location. The idea behind the proposed meetings is that office professionals will be able to meet to exchange ideas that will help them perform their jobs more efficiently.

Charley is accustomed to setting up meetings that his supervisor will be leading, but this is the first time he has had to do this sort of thing on his own. His supervisor tells him that she is confident he can handle this. Charley reserves the room for the first meeting and notifies the appropriate office professionals that there will be a meeting they need to attend. He also orders snacks for the meeting. During the first meeting, though, none of the office professionals knows why they have been called together. However, several comment that they are glad to have a "snack break" and a chance to get away from their desks for a while. These comments lead some of the office professionals to relay stories of their experiences with various office personnel. To Charley's dismay, the meeting slowly turned into a gossip session with office professionals griping about some of the office professionals they support.

Charley sat by helplessly, not knowing what he should do.

Although answers may vary, here are some suggested responses:

1. What could Charley have done before the meeting to make sure the office professionals came to the meeting prepared to stay on focus?

   Charley should have sent out an agenda ahead of schedule. He should have notified the appropriate office professionals and stated clearly why the meeting was being called. He could even have asked them to come prepared to discuss the items noted on the agenda. He should have made it clear that while he was leading the meeting, he wanted input from everyone.

2. What could Charley have done during the meeting to keep things on track?

   As the meeting leader, there are guidelines Charley should have followed. Once he had made the purpose of the meeting clear ahead of time, it was his responsibility to reiterate the purpose at the beginning of the meeting. He also should have let the participants know the objectives of the meeting—what must be accomplished at the meeting and what needs to be done after the meeting. In addition, Charley should have stuck to the agenda. If any of the participants strayed from the agenda, the leader is responsible for sensitively but firmly bringing them back to it. He should have kept the discussion moving toward the objectives and outcomes determined prior to the meeting.

3. If Charley felt unprepared for leading the meeting, how should he have handled this when he originally discussed it with the supervisor?

   If Charley did not feel comfortable in setting up and leading a meeting, he should have discussed this with his supervisor and asked for some suggestions from her in handling this task—especially since this was his first time in this role. In addition, if Charley did not feel comfortable presiding over the meeting, he could have met in advance with one of the other office professionals and had that person preside over the meeting.

4. Since the office professionals seemed to enjoy the meeting, would you consider this an effective meeting? List your reasoning.

   This is not an effective meeting. An effective meeting is one in which:
   - There is a definite need for the meeting
   - The purpose is stated and clearly understood by all participants
   - The appropriate people are in attendance at the meeting
   - An agenda is prepared and adhered to
   - All members participate
   - There are outcomes achieved as a result of the meeting

Although there was a need for the meeting, and perhaps the appropriate people were in attendance, none of the other criteria were met.

ACHIEVEMENT TEST
PART 6 (Chapters 19–20)

PART A—TRUE-FALSE

Directions: The answer to each of the following statements is either true or false. Indicate your choice in the Answers column by circling **T** for a true statement or **F** for a false statement. Each correct answer is worth 1 point.

Answers

T, C19, p. 515	1. Before you begin looking for a job, you need to be clear about what your long-range career goals are.
F, C19, p. 515	2. A signed advertisement includes the name of the person to whom you will report.
T, C19, p. 516	3. Salary information about particular jobs is available on the Internet.
F, C19, p. 516	4. When going through a private employment agency to find a job, the applicant always pays a fee.
T, C19, p. 519	5. A temporary agency may be a source of job information.
F, C19, p. 521	6. The letter of application may be two pages in length.
T, C19, p. 523	7. The appropriate salutation to use when addressing a letter of application is "Ladies and Gentlemen" if you do not have the name or title of anyone in the organization.
T, C19, p. 528	8. It is acceptable to list volunteer jobs or leadership positions on a resume if you have limited work experience.
F, C19, p. 529	9. It is acceptable to use personal pronouns when preparing a resume.
F, C19, p. 529	10. When preparing a resume for electronic scanning, use boldface type and italics.
F, C19, p. 532	11. It is acceptable to be five minutes late for an interview.
F, C19, p. 536	12. Females should carry both a briefcase and a handbag to the interview.
T, C19, p. 538	13. It is usually acceptable to follow up after an interview with two or three contacts to the individual who interviewed you.
T, C19, p. 540	14. When you begin a new job, ask how you will be evaluated.
F, C19, p. 546	15. It is appropriate to criticize your employer or the company on an exit interview.
T, C20, p. 557	16. Power may be based on the leader's knowledge.
T, C20, p. 560	17. Effective leaders are reliable and predictable.
F, C20, p. 564	18. Tactical planning is the process by which the ideas from strategic thinking are translated into an action format.
T, C20, p. 564	19. When determining span of control, it is important to consider the leadership philosophy of the organization.
F, C20, p. 568	20. When interviewing a prospective applicant, it is appropriate to ask if he or she is married.
F, C20, p. 568	21. In the interview process, it is appropriate to ask a prospective applicant the date of his or her birth.
T, C20, p. 569	22. Organizations may assign a new employee a mentor to help train the employee.
F, C20, p. 572	23. Employee performance should be evaluated on a yearly or twice yearly basis only.
T, C20, p. 574	24. Giving recognition to an employee is a form of motivation.
T, C20, p. 576	25. An effective leader is also a teacher.

PART B—MATCHING

Directions: In the Answers column, write the letter of the item in Column 1 that defines the statement in Column 2. Each correct answer is worth 2 points.

Column 1	Answers	Column 2
A. control measures	I, C19, p. 518	1. The process of identifying and establishing a group of acquaintances, friends, and relatives who can assist you in the job search process
B. projection		
C. chronological		
D. portfolio	C, C19, p. 524	2. A resume format in which you list your work experience and education in reverse date order
E. leadership		
F. management	J, C19, p. 524	3. A resume format in which experience is organized into categories
G. planning		
H. span of control	D, C19, p. 532	4. A compilation of samples of your work
I. networking	O, C19, p. 543	5. The state of being bound emotionally or intellectually to some course of action
J. functional		
K. job analysis	E, C20, p. 557	6. The process of persuading others to take action that is consistent with the group's purpose
L. job enrichment		
M. strategic thinking	F, C20, p. 557	7. The performance of tasks or activities that are necessary, such as planning, organizing, leading, and controlling
N. empowering		
O. commitment		
	N, C20, p. 560	8. Providing employees access to information that will help them do their jobs better
	M, C20, p. 561	9. Process used to help individuals envision goals
	G, C20, p. 563	10. Setting goals and objectives for the organization
	H, C20, p. 564	11. The number of employees who are directly supervised by one person
	K, C20, p. 566	12. List of tasks for a specific job and the personal characteristics necessary to perform the tasks
	A, C20, p. 570	13. Using procedures, budgets, and data to measure performance
	B, C20, p. 572	14. The phenomenon of transferring our problems to others
	L, C20, p. 574	15. Giving employees a greater variety of duties to perform

PART C—SHORT ANSWER

Directions: For each of the following statements, provide the answers required. The point value is given for each statement. Place your answers on a separate sheet of paper; you may want to use the computer in answering these questions.

1. What are the purposes of the letter of application? (8 points) (C19, p. 521)

   - Introducing you to the organization
   - Providing general information about your skills
   - Selling your skills—letting the reader know that you have something to offer the organization
   - Transmitting your resume

2. List the parts of a resume. (5 points) (C19, pp. 524 and 528)

   The resume should include six parts, which are:

   - Resume heading
   - Objective
   - Relevant skills
   - Employment history
   - Education
   - Professional accomplishments

   Another section that may be added is references. However, this section is not essential on the resume itself.

3. What are the purposes and advantages of an electronic resume? (4 points) (C19, p. 530)

Organizations are using computer tracking systems to search through resumes and narrow the search to a few individuals. In addition, an electronic resume has these advantages for the individual.

- You can send your resume by email to a prospective employer.
- You can add your resume to online databases—a free service offered by career-related sites.
- You prove to the prospective employer that you are computer literate.

These guidelines should be followed:

- Do not use bold, italics, underlining.
- Use a basic font such as Times New Roman or Courier.
- Use a standard typesize (12-point).
- Use a standard resume format.
- Do not use any abbreviations.

4. List five guidelines that should be used when being interviewed by a team. (5 points) (C19, pp. 532–533)

The student may list any five of the following guidelines:

- Pay careful attention to each individual's name as he or she is introduced.
- As each person asks a question, focus on that person. Listen carefully and answer the question succinctly.
- When you ask a question, ask it of the group unless one person has said something on which you wish to follow up.
- Make eye contact with all individuals if the question or statement is meant for the entire group.
- If you find yourself getting nervous, glance occasionally at the person or persons who have given you positive feedback—the ones who have a friendly face, open body language, and positive reactions to your responses.
- Thank the group after the interview is over.

5. What should a follow-up letter include? (8 points) (C19, p. 538)

- A thank-you for the opportunity to interview
- A recap of your skills and abilities
- A statement of your continued interest in the job
- A reminder of the next steps you agreed on in the interview, such as when the decision is going to be made

6. List the tasks of leadership. (7 points) (C20, p. 561)

- Envisioning goals
- Affirming values
- Managing
- Motivating
- Achieving unity
- Explaining and teaching
- Renewing

7. When recruiting employees, list the three major tools used for screening and selection. (3 points) (C20, p. 568)

- Written application
- Personal interview
- Testing procedures

8. Explain the role the effective leader has in an employee's objective setting process. (5 points) (C20, p. 574)

The effective leader helps employees establish challenging, measurable objectives. Once these objectives are established, the effective leader helps the employees achieve them. Doing so requires follow-through and planning on the part of the leader/supervisor. The supervisor must not only know what the objectives are but also follow up to see that the employees have achieved them.

PART D—OPTIONAL CASE

Directions: Select two of your classmates to work with on this case. Respond to the items at the end of the case. (20 points)

Cynthia Mandorf has completed her associate degree in office systems. Cynthia was an average student in college, making B's and C's in her courses. She enjoys working on a computer and has proficiency in several software packages, including word processing, spreadsheet, and scheduling software. She keyboards at a rate of 60 wpm. Cynthia chose to take two psychology courses as electives because she is very interested in understanding the emotional behavior and characteristics of individuals and groups. She thoroughly enjoyed the psychology courses and made an A in both courses. She would like to work in an environment where she can interact with a number of people each day. She has thought of working in either a college/university or a medical setting. Cynthia picked one university, one college, and two hospitals in her city where she feels she would like to work. She does not know whether they have any openings; however, she decides to visit the human resource departments in all locations and ask if there are openings. Due to her excellent communication skills, her "walk-in" approach results in two job interviews—one at the university and one at a hospital. Her work experience includes two previous jobs—one a full-time job as a waitperson in the summer between high school and college, the other a part-time job as a clerk in a department store.

In preparing her resume, Cynthia listed as her objective, "A position as an administrative assistant." She did not list her two jobs on the resume; she did not consider them relevant. On the hospital interview, she was five minutes late. She apologized to the receptionist, stating that she had trouble finding a parking space. When she was asked in the interview why she wanted to work for the hospital, she stated that she loved working with people. She then talked about the psychology courses she had taken and how much she believed she had learned about human behavior. When she was asked what her goals were, she stated that she wanted to continue her education and become a social worker some day. When she was asked why the hospital should hire her, she again talked about how much she enjoyed working with people. The human resource director stated that she would let her know within the next week. Cynthia liked the HR director and felt that she had made a good impression. In the follow-up letter that she wrote to the hospital, she stated that she felt she would make an excellent administrative assistant. However, she failed to point out why she thought she would be excellent; she did not list any of her skills that would benefit the hospital. As Cynthia critiqued her interview performance, she felt she had handled the interview well. She did realize that she should not have been late and promised herself that she would not let that happen again.

The interview with the university was two days after the interview at the hospital. Cynthia made a point to be five minutes early to the interview. As she talked with the human resource director, she told her that she was interested in the position but that she was also applying for other positions. She again stressed her interest in working with people when asked why she wanted to work for the university. She did, however, point out that she had good computer, software, and keyboarding skills. When asked about an ethical dilemma that she had faced, Cynthia told the HR director that one time a student who sat next to her in psychology wanted to copy from her work as they were taking a test. She moved her paper so that the student could see her answers and let him copy. She felt terrible about it after it happened and decided that she would never do it again and she didn't. The interviewer did not make any comments after Cynthia relayed the story; she wondered what the interviewer thought. When asked what she knew about the university, Cynthia responded that one of her friends was a graduate. When asked by the HR director if she had any questions, Cynthia asked, "What is the salary?" The HR director told her that a decision would be made in two weeks. Cynthia sent a follow-up letter thanking the director.

Cynthia felt she had a good chance of being offered both jobs. She liked both of the interviewers and thought they liked her. However, two weeks passed and she heard nothing. She felt depressed and wondered what she had done wrong.

Answers will vary; here are suggested responses.

- Critique the way in which Cynthia conducted her job search, her interview techniques, and her follow-up.
  Cynthia chose only one way to find a job—through walk-in. She should have taken the time to search through the newspaper, the Internet, and to talk with her friends about job possibilities. Her search process was too narrow. In the interview, rather than talk about her skills as an administrative assistant, she chose to focus on her interest in people. Certainly, as an administrative assistant it is important to have good communication and human relation skills. Cynthia's mistake was that she made this one area the focus rather than point out all the skills that she has. She did send a follow-up letter; however, again, she failed to point out her skills. She certainly should have taken the opportunity in the letter to point out her computer skills, keyboarding skills, and so forth. She only sent one follow-up letter; she could have also called the organizations.

- List her strengths and her weaknesses.

Strengths
Cynthia has an associate degree; she has proficiency in several software packages, including word processing, spreadsheet, and scheduling software. She keyboards at an acceptable rate (60 wpm). She has good communication and human relation skills.

Although she has no office experience, she has held two jobs—a waitperson and a clerk, which demonstrates her work ethic.

Weaknesses

Cynthia has no office experience; however, she can focus on her associate degree when interviewing. She seems more interested in social work than in office work; she needs to be clear on her career goals. If she plans to use office work to finance her schooling to become a social worker, she should not point that out in an interview. Her planning skills in the interview process were weak; she did not plan the search process well. She also gave little attention to planning for the interview; she did not research the organizations where she was applying.

- What mistakes did she make?

    —In preparing her resume, her objective is not specific enough. She did not list her two jobs on the resume.

    —She was five minutes late for one interview.

    —The reason she gave for wanting to work in the hospital was weak.

    —She led the interviewer to believe that she was mainly interested in becoming a social worker rather than an administrative assistant.

    —She gave an ineffective reason that the hospital should hire her.

    —Her follow-up letters were ineffective; she should have: thanked the interviewer for his or her time, recapped her skills and abilities, stated why she was interested in the job, and reminded the interviewer of when she would be hearing from him or her.

    —The ethical dilemma that Cynthia presented to the university was not the best one that she could have chosen. It would have been better to pick an ethical dilemma that occurred on one of her jobs.

    —Cynthia did not appear to know much about the university; her response was that one of her friends graduated from the university. She should have known such things as the programs that were offered, the number of students, its directions, whether or not it offers graduate programs, and so forth.

    —She responded inappropriately when asked if she had any questions. Salary should never be the first question. During the initial interview, you should avoid questions about salary, benefits, vacation time, and so forth. In other words, you want to avoid questions that relate to what the company can do for you and ask questions that demonstrate your interest in learning more about the company.

KEY TO SIMULATED OFFICE APPLICATION

In the Applications Workbook on pages 144–146, there is a five-day simulated office activity. The activity is designed to engage the student in critical thinking by giving enough information to perform the job while at the same time requiring the student to think through each situation. There is no one answer to each activity; suggestions are given here. The student works for People First International. The supervisor is Juan Menendez, vice president of International Operations. The student supervises one office professional, Roger VanDorn.

You may choose not to grade this activity but use it as a culminating critical thinking and team building activity with two or three students working together on the project. Then a class discussion might take place about how each situation was handled. You also may choose to use it as a final exam.

KEY FOR DAY 1—TUESDAY, APRIL 11

SOA2

TO BE DONE	TO BE DELEGATED (ROGER)
1. Compose three letters.	1. Make appointments; Roger is to prepare a memo detailing when the appointments are scheduled; once the memo is approved by you, it will go to Mr. Menendez.
2. Review appointments that Roger has set up.	2. Complete filing.
3. Make flight and hotel reservations for Paris; prepare itinerary.	3. Prepare report.
4. Prepare memo for Jean Boudreaux in Paris office; prepare fax cover sheet.	
5. IAAP Conference planning	

Nothing can be delegated to Roger for IAAP. That is not the agreement that has been made with Mr. Menendez. It would not be ethical to delegate this work to Roger. (The student may suggest that the administrative assistant talk with Mr. Menendez about the possibility of delegating some of the IAAP tasks to Roger. This is a judgment call; the administrative assistant has already received considerable support from Mr. Menendez.)

Itinerary

The student is to use the Internet in getting times for the flights to Paris. The itinerary form followed should be one similar to that shown in the text on page 467.

Memo to Jean Boudreaux

The memo should be placed on a memo form and should give the exact flight times. A request should be made for someone to meet them at the airport, with Jean informing the administrative assistant who that person will be. A fax cover sheet is to be prepared.

Day 2—Wednesday, April 12

Roger has some performance problems; however, the administrative assistant has not talked with him about these problems—nor has he been given any information about how he is to be evaluated. An evaluation form is to be prepared along with an outline of the performance issues that need to be discussed with Roger.

Evaluation Form

An evaluation form is given in Chapter 19 on pages 541–542; the student may use a similar format.

Outline of Performance Issues

Evaluation guidelines are given in Chapter 20; the student should review these guidelines. Issues to be discussed include:

- Meeting deadlines (failed to get filing done on time)
- Late for work, with no explanation for lateness
- Lack of understanding of the filing system (cannot find materials)
- Spends too much time engaged in chitchat with coworkers
- Poor attitude (upset when given a large amount of work)

The administrative assistant must realize that he or she has made mistakes also. Roger has not been told how he will be evaluated and has not been talked with as problems have arisen. In the session with Roger, the administrative assistant should:

- Be fair—give Roger credit for what he has done right.
- Listen to what Roger has to say.
- Allow adequate time for the evaluation—set aside at least an hour, with no interruptions allowed.
- Help Roger establish obtainable objectives; for example, Roger may need some training on the filing system.
- Go over the evaluation form with Roger; explain how and when he will be formally evaluated.

The administrative assistant should also commit to himself or herself that daily or weekly evaluation will occur. For example, when Roger does not perform well, it should be noted and discussed with Roger. When he does perform well, praise should be extended.

Day 3—Thursday, April 13

- The student is to write two letters:
One to Edwina Bos, asking her to speak at the Detroit Economic Conference on directions for the Detroit Public Schools to be held on December 10. The presentation is to be no more than one hour in length, with the time frame being from 10 a.m. to 11 a.m.

  The second letter is to be written to a new client, Mr. Wayne Grant, thanking him for his business and suggesting a luncheon meeting on Tuesday, May 2, at Brookhaven Country Club to discuss any training needs that he might have.

- The administrative assistant has the evaluation talk with Roger. After the talk, Roger has a long conversation with his friend Paul. The administrative assistant wonders if Roger is discussing his evaluation with the friend and wonders if there should be a talk with Roger about it.

  The administrative assistant should not make the assumption that Roger is talking with the friend about the evaluation. However, if the problem with Roger spending too much time chitchatting continues, the administrative assistant should talk with him about that issue. It has already been discussed once, and Roger should understand that it is a serious issue that is getting in the way of him having the time to perform his work. In other words, the administrative assistant should deal with the problem (if there is one), not make an assumption that may or may not be true.

Day 4—Friday, April 14

The administrative assistant has several problem situations. The student is to explain how these situations should have been handled.

- A caller is upset; Mr. Menendez is not in; the caller refers the call to Ms. Bauer. Ms. Bauer talks with the individual and then asks to talk with Mr. Menendez when he gets in; you send an email about her request to Mr. Menendez. Mr. Menendez does not read his email and is upset that you have not told him that Ms. Bauer wants to see him.

  Even though Mr. Menendez closed his door immediately upon his arrival, you should have informed him about the situation of the upset caller and Ms. Bauer wanting to see him. You could have called him by telephone or knocked on his door with the message. Once the problem has occurred, you should apologize to Mr. Menendez, stating that you did not want to disturb him and that you sent an email. However, in the future you will notify him in person immediately.

- Ms. Engleton calls the administrative assistant at 1 p.m. asking for information that is in the files. The administrative assistant puts her on hold to get the information. Then there is an interruption by Mr. Menendez, and before the administrative assistant returns to the phone, Ms. Engleton has hung up.

  You should have told Ms. Engleton that you would call back within 10 minutes with the information that was needed. Do not put anyone on hold while checking the files; it usually takes more time than anticipated, even without an interruption. However, since Ms. Engleton was put on hold, you should have called her back immediately when it was discovered that she had hung up. You should not wait for Ms. Engleton to call you. You also should apologize to Ms. Engleton.

- You should talk with Roger about company policy stating that an employee cannot make personal copies on the office copier.
- The administrative assistant is to research effective communication techniques on the Internet and prepare an outline for the IAAP Effective Communication Conference. Outlines will vary, but these topics may be included:

   I. Verbal Communication
      A. Reduce Communication Barriers
      B. Watch your Nonverbal Communication
   II. Written Communication
      A. Writing Effective Letters
      B. Writing Effective Email and Memorandums
      C. Writing Effective Reports

- You should follow company procedure in informing the appropriate person that you are working late; notifying the security staff is standard procedure. You should take these precautions:

   — Notify someone at your home that you are working late. Call the person before you leave, notifying him or her that you are on your way home.
   — If you drive to work, walk to your car with someone else if possible. Or ask an individual from the security staff to accompany you to your car. Have your car keys ready to unlock your car. Lock your car immediately after getting in.
   — Situate yourself near others who are working late if possible.
   — Work next to a telephone and have emergency numbers handy.
   — Keep all doors to your office locked while working.
   — If you hear strange noises, call for help. Do not investigate on your own.

Day 5—Monday, April 17

- An upset coworker calls asking that the administrative assistant discuss a matter with her immediately. The administrative assistant agrees to meet the coworker.

   Debra, the coworker, should be told that she should report the incident to Human Resources immediately. Before doing so, she should write down the situation exactly as it occurred, giving the date and time. She should also attempt to detail the other incidences that have occurred, giving approximate dates and times. If Human Resources does not handle the situation, Debra may file an EEOC complaint or decide to look for another job. She should also make clear to the man that she has absolutely no interest in him.

   You should tell Mr. Menendez that a coworker called with a very important issue; explain to him that it had to do with sexual harassment and that you advised the employee to talk with Human Resources. You should also tell him that you will let Roger know how he can reach you when you leave the office in the future. You do not need to tell Roger where you are going; you can give him a telephone number where he may reach you.

- The administrative assistant has a talk with Roger about his making personal copies on the office copier. Roger doesn't understand why he can't make copies for his class since the administrative assistant is making copies for IAAP use. He sees both as professional development and believes that the company should be fair by giving all employees the same opportunity.

   You should listen carefully to Roger's feelings, telling him that you understand the distinction may be hard to make. However, here are some considerations. He is taking classes to get an engineering degree and a new job outside the company. You cannot expect a company to support professional growth that leads to the person leaving the company. Also, he did not ask permission to copy the materials; if he thought he had a legitimate copying case, he should have asked permission. And IAAP is an organization that helps the larger community by providing for professional growth for office support personnel throughout the community. People First is committed to professional growth and to community support.